LAST TRAIN TO PARADISE

NEW AND SELECTED POEMS

MARTHA SILANO

Distributed by Independent Publishers Group
Chicago

©2025 Martha Silano
No part of this book may be used or reproduced in any manner without written permission except in the case of brief quotations embodied in critical articles and reviews. Please direct inquiries to:

Saturnalia Books
2816 North Kent Rd.
Broomall, PA 19008
info@saturnaliabooks.com

ISBN: 978-1947817-84-5 (print), 978-1947817-85-2 (ebook)
Library of Congress Control Number: 2025930670

Cover art and book design by Robin Vuchnich

Distributed by:
Independent Publishing Group
814 N. Franklin St.
Chicago, IL 60610
800-888-4741

For Langdon Cook

CONTENTS

FORWARD
THE MORNS ARE MEEKER – BY DIANE SEUSS   1

NEW POEMS   1
THE BLOOMING   3
I WAS TRYING TO WEIGH DARKNESS   4
WHY I'D LIKE TO MEET MY MAKER   5
WHAT IS TOO MUCH   7
WHEN THIS BOAT MY BODY   8
POSTPARTUM PSYCHOSIS   9
BLESSED ARE THEY THAT MOURN   11
AND YET IT MOVES   13
WHAT ISN'T BROKEN   15
WHAT I WISHED FOR   17
THE WEEDS   19
SONG   20
WHEN I BEGAN TO DIG   22
THE VITAL QUESTION   24
POETRY,   25
ARS POETICA   27
I SOLD MY PREDICATES,   29
THE BALD EAGLES OF SEWARD PARK   30
THERE'S SO MUCH TO ADMIRE   32
THE SIGNS WERE CLEAR   35
WHEN WISPY CLOUDS DRIFT THROUGH SPARSELY WOODED MOUNTAINS   37
DASHING   39
THE DOE OUTSIDE OUR BACK DOOR   41
AND THE ROAD IS LIKE A CAVE WITH YELLOW WALLS   42
IN ANOTHER LIFE   43
LAST TRAIN TO PARADISE   44

BUYING AND SELLING	45
THE WHOLE VAGINA EXPERIENCE	47
NOW WE COME TO TICKS AND TOCKS	49
POEM FOR MY DAUGHTER ON HER 18TH BIRTHDAY	51
THE PRECISE MODE OF FAILURE COULD NOT BE REPLICATED,	53
JUST DON'T THINK ABOUT WATERFALLS	54
FONDEST MEMORIES FROM THE LOCKED WARD	56
EAT PREY, LOVE	58
I'M NOT SURE WHY I DECIDED	60

FROM: WHAT THE TRUTH TASTES LIKE (1998) — 61

THE MAN WHO SLEPT IN MY BED	63
LADYBUG	65
SWEET RED PEPPERS, SUN-DRIEDS, THE HEARTS OF ARTICHOKES	66
THE TABLE OF LOSSES	67
THE MOON	68
JENNIFER'S PEACHES CARDINAL HUME FOR THE PRIESTS AT WESTMINSTER CATHEDRAL	69
HOLLY HOCK BAKERY'S MOVING TO MADISON VALLEY	70
THE SAUSAGE PARADE	71
MY HOUR WITH JORIE GRAHAM	73
WHAT THE GRAD STUDENTS SAID	76
JUST DON'T WRITE ANY POEMS ABOUT NIAGARA FALLS	78
WHAT I MEANT TO SAY BEFORE I SAID 'SO LONG'	80
AT THE SHOREBIRD FESTIVAL: GRAYS HARBOR COUNTY, WASHINGTON	82
SUCH A WAY TO GO	85
THEY'RE PROHIBITED BY CITY ORDINANCE	86
IN THAT OTHER UNIVERSE	87
TO THE WOMAN WHO, WHEN I WENT TO HEAT MY PIZZA IN THE OFFICE MICROWAVE, ASKED ME, "WHO ARE YOU?"	88

MEN OF THE STONE AGE HAD NO USE FOR FRACTIONS	89
TOO SMALL FOR INTELLECT, BIG ENOUGH FOR LOVE	90
TOWARD AN UNDERSTANDING OF MY SO-CALLED CALLING	91
THE 1238 CHERRY AVENUE CREDO	93
SPELLCHECK CHANGES *SILANO* TO *SALINE*	94

FROM: BLUE POSITIVE (2006) 95

BLUE POSITIVE	97
THIS IS NOT THE LAST POEM ABOUT PEARS	99
MOTHER OF PEACE	101
MY WORDS	103
MY MAN WITH HIS FLY REEL EYES	104
TRAVELER'S LAMENT	105
SALVAGING JUST MIGHT LEAD TO SALVATION	106
DEFINE MEDICAL TERMINOLOGY AND CONDITIONS ASSOCIATED WITH CONCEPTION	111
CROWN OF SONNETS FOR A SON	114
GETTING KICKED BY A FETUS	118
SONG FOR A NEWBORN	120
HARBORVIEW	121
EXPLAINING CURRENT EVENTS TO A ONE-YEAR OLD	123
FOUR A.M.	125
MY SON ASKS *WHAT'S A TORRENT?*	126
HIS FAVORITE COLOR IS GREEN	127
FORGETFULNESS THE GREAT BRONCHIAL TREE FROM WHICH I'M SWINGING	129
LOW TIDE WALK WITH MARY GRACE	131
THE FORBIDDEN FRUIT	132
AMANITA CALYPTRATA	134
BEGGING TO DIFFER	136
I CAN'T WRITE	138

WHAT LITTLE GIRLS ARE MADE OF	140
VICTORIA'S SECRET	142

FROM: THE LITTLE OFFICE OF THE IMMACULATE CONCEPTION (2011) — 143

MY PLACE IN THE UNIVERSE	145
I LIVE ON MILK STREET	147
OURS	149
WHAT I WILL TELL THE ALIENS	151
IN PRAISE OF NOT GETTING	153
ODE TO IMAGINATION	156
THE LITTLE OFFICE OF THE IMMACULATE CONCEPTION	158
AFTER READING THERE MIGHT BE AN INFINITE NUMBER OF DIMENSIONS	160
POOR BANISHED CHILDREN OF EVE	162
LOVE	164
THIS PARENTING THING	166
MORE WAVES MAY FOLLOW	170
HOW TO SEW	172
EASTER VISIT	174
IT'S ALL GRAVY	176

FROM: RECKLESS LOVELY (2014) — 179

PALE BLUE DOT	181
LA GIOCONDA	183
ODE TO FRIDA KAHLO'S EYEBROWS	186
SUMMONS AND PETITION FOR NAME CHANGE	188
WOLVES KEEP IN TOUCH BY HOWLING	189
LEONARDO DA VINCI'S GRAN CAVALLO	190
THE POET IS THE PRIEST OF THE INVISIBLE	192
WHAT FALLS FROM TRUCKS, FROM THE LIPS OF SAVIORS	193

FROM: GRAVITY ASSIST (2019) — 195
SONG OF WEIGHTS AND MEASUREMENTS — 197
INSTEAD OF A FATHER — 199
REPORT YOUR UNUSUAL PHENOMENON — 200
MY ENVIRONS — 202
GERBILS IN SPACE — 203
ODE TO AUTOCORRECT — 205
NEARLY EVERY SONGBIRD ON EARTH IS EATING PLASTIC — 207
STILL LIFE WITH MOTORCYCLE REVVING, WAILING SIREN, AMERICAN GOLDFINCH TRILL — 209
BUMBLEBEES ARE MADE OF ASH — 211
SPACE PROBE PANTOUM — 212
PEACH GLOSA — 214
BREAK-AWAY EFFECT — 216

FROM: THIS ONE WE CALL OURS (2024) — 219
WHAT THEY SAID — 221
ONCE, — 223
TWO HUNDRED MILLION YEARS AGO THIS WAS ALL A SEA FLOOR, — 225
DURING THE CRETACEOUS OUR COUNTRY WAS DIVIDED FOR SIXTY MILLION YEARS — 226
NO RAIN — 228
WHEN WE SAY IT'S THE LITTLE THINGS — 230
OH, AUTOLYSIS — 231
LETTER TO A POST-APOCALYPTIC COCKROACH — 233
POEM WRITTEN ONE HUNDRED YARDS FROM MY MOTHER'S GRAVE — 235
SELF-PORTRAIT AS SOUTHERN RESIDENT ORCA — 236
TIME AND DISTANCE — 238
FAILED ATTEMPT AT MYTHMAKING — 239
SOUL RECKONING — 240

THAT SUMMER	242
EVERYTHING ENDS	243

FROM: TERMINAL SURREAL (2025)   245

FLYING RATS	247
WHAT'S TERRIBLE	249
POSSIBLE DIAGNOSIS	250
ORDERS OF OPERATION	252
SINCE YOU'RE ALIVE	254
WHEN I LEARN *CATASTROPHICALLY*	256
TO-DO LIST	258
ABECEDARIAN WITH ALS	259
I DIDN'T UNDERSTAND KEATS'S "ODE TO A NIGHTINGALE"	260
TERMINAL SURREAL	262
SELF-ELEGIES	263
POEM ON MY SON'S TWENTY-THIRD BIRTHDAY	266
A POEM ABOUT TWINFLOWER	268
MY NINETEEN-YEAR-OLD DAUGHTER IS MY PERSONAL ASSISTANT, YOU ARE MUCH MORE THAN THIS BODY	269 270
AUTHOR BIO	273
ACKNOWLEDGMENTS	275
POEMS IN ANTHOLOGIES	277

FORWARD

THE MORNS ARE MEEKER – BY DIANE SEUSS

Some of the most important poems, the ones that are most lasting, are those written under conditions of urgency. Martha Silano's work has always struck me as such, but the tenor of the urgency has changed. Her early poems are urgent in their exuberance for language, for the sheer ecstasy of the power to call out the names of things. The world's concrete details are nearly too much for her. She's fevered; she must impart them to us in dizzying, often ironic, sometimes hilarious lists. Names of places: Joy, Bromide, Mustang, Homer, Love County, Lone Grove, Sugarville, and Muse. Jobs she's done: "Once it was a cornfield, / sixteen hours a day in a moving cage, reaching // for tassels. I've picked cherries, scooped / pickles, sold knives and rakes and // rolls that fell to the floor…" Factoids: The temperature range on the moon. The ammonites, who eat their young, and their shells that contain their entire life histories. The fact that during the Cretaceous, "clams were the size of small area rugs, / turtles as big as Dodge Darts." Desserts, from her poem "Holly Hock Bakery's Moving to Madison Valley": "So she's leaving us, dear Holly, for blacker forests, / for banana cream more creamy, for exponentially irresistible tarts. // So long, loganberry seven layer. Bon voyage, apricot chiffon. / Going, going, cinnamon buckle, gone." She writes to her child in utero, "today you weigh six potato chips." She addresses him, as a newborn, as "Oh my Double Thick Pork Chop."

The wonders unfold and gain nuance with the arrival of each new collection. In "This is Not the Last Poem about Pears," from *Blue Positive,* she describes petals falling from a pear tree, "When they fall they leave behind / hundreds of parasols not unlike / the ones you saw as you gazed into pond water / under a microscope," merging her naturalist inclinations with her lyric eye, the expansive with the infinitesimal. One poem is a paean to her young son's favorite color, green, "like just-before-blooming phlox," "the big square Missoula Sioux City Throgsneck Bridge / along the freeway with horsetail astragalus vetch," "mama calliope warming her eggs," "[t]he semi-spicate the glume-ful the spikelike the membranous / [t]

he shallowly bifid the twisted the sticky the hollow," "[h]is world's hickory buckeye slippery elm," "[s]o much of his world so much of this world // even where plowed where fires even in cities / a hispid persistence …" What a rush, what a Whitman-yawping, Ginsberg-howling praise song!

But Martha's work offers more than the pleasures of the senses. Its urgency can transport us into the deepest, most purple shadows, especially when addressing what she calls in a newer poem, "The whole vagina experience," right up there with another, "This Parenting Thing." The epigraph for "Harborview" comes, fittingly, from Sylvia Plath: "By the roots of my hair some god got hold of me," the trope that fuels Martha's female-identifying, tongue-in-cheek litany: "By the roots of my hair, by the reinforced elastic / of my floral Bravado bra, by the fraying strands // of my blue-checked briefs." The poem's reportage quickly becomes harrowing, as the speaker's post-partum mental health becomes an emergency. "Some god's got me thinking my milk's poison, unfit / for a hungry child … as if the god who's got hold of me doesn't want me / well, doesn't want my rapid-fire brain to slow, // wants this ride for as long as it lasts, wants to take it / to its over-Niagara-in-a-barrel end, which is where // this god is taking me, one rung at a time, one ambulance, / one EMT strapping me in …" In Silano's poem, unlike Plath's, written some forty years earlier, the godhead is female, dragging a body into raw experience and pulling it up by its hair into a ravaged salvation. "[S]ome god got hold of me, / shook and shook me long and hard, she also brought me back." Newer poems, "Postpartum Psychosis" and "Fondest Memories from the Locked Ward," concentrate more fully on the brutal and tender details of going in-patient. "When we love something, / we say we're a pig in mud. When we're out of our minds, // we say we're coo-coo for Cocoa Puffs. When I was an insect / banging against the rafters, when I believed I could fly, / they got out the giant fly swatter." These poems take poetry itself on a rare excursion into the hazard zone of women's reproductive and mental health. They inhabit the far reaches of lyric intensity.

As we move through this comprehensive new and selected, we also witness Martha taking on American poetry's social hierarchies, its class and caste system. If you know, you know—an uncomfortable lunch with a famous writer, feeling clumsy, and unsophisticated, and uninformed. Gleaning, from the Great Ones, the subjects that matter and the subjects that don't, as in a poem titled after a bit of advice from Richard Hugo, "Just Don't Write Any Poems About Niagara Falls," which opens a litany of all the things "we" don't care about, like "your childhood: gargantuan zucchinis, / ailing mimosas, the day your father sliced // your beach ball with his pocket knife…" It reminds me of Auden's reputed comment, on leaving a reading, "Who the hell cares about Anne Sexton's grandmother?" One of my favorites in this mode, "What the Grad Students Said," tells of the experience of having one's manuscript judged for a prize. "And all your poems should be as good / as this first one, which not only stood out // like a tilt-a-whirl on a flatbed broken down / along I-5, but reminded us of the words // we hate, like any compound adjective / and *scrunch*." There's humor, but also an undercurrent of pain, while still managing to get at the sheer absurdity of it all. "In other words, you weren't a finalist, runner-up, semi-finalist, // 22nd or even 55th in line, but you were definitely / one of the 67 entrants!" Martha names it, and expounds on it, and in this naming, the hierarchical rafters start to shudder.

I want to step back from the poems for a bit and address the life. Martha was born and raised in Metuchen, New Jersey. After graduating from public school, she went to Grinnell College, receiving a Bachelor's in English, and ultimately did graduate work at the University of Washington. Her love of poetry began in second grade, when her teacher, Mrs. Everett, recited an Emily Dickinson poem to the class. It was the tremendous ditty, "The morns are meeker than they were."

The morns are meeker than they were -
The nuts are getting brown -
The berry's cheek is plumper -
The rose is out of town.

The maple wears a gayer scarf -
The field a scarlet gown -
Lest I sh'd be old-fashioned
I'll put a trinket on.

Martha started writing a diary at age nine, and never stopped. She now has hundreds of scrawl-filled notebooks. As a young girl, she wrote poems, but showed no one. Like many of us, she felt insecure about her work, and did not step into a creative writing class until she was in her middle-twenties. When her children were young, she took them to playgrounds, and wrote. To science museums, and wrote. To zoos, and wrote. At the University of Washington, where she received her MFA, she encountered David Wagoner, whose influence, she says, changed her life. "He told me I needed a 5-beat line. He said my music was all messed up." She applied what she learned about metrics from Wagoner to writing her first sonnet. Finally, at age thirty-eight, she put together a manuscript, *What the Truth Tastes Like,* which won the Potato Eyes Foundation Prize from Nightshade Press.

In 2023, Martha began experiencing physical symptoms that concerned her. "I googled ALS," she tells me, "which sounded about right, but no one would believe me." In late November of that year, Martha was, indeed, diagnosed with ALS, amyotrophic lateral sclerosis, a neuro-degenerative illness that impacts movement, speech, eating, and breathing. When I learned of her illness, it struck me as a particularly cruel set of symptoms, given her lifelong love of moving, with athleticism and exuberance, through the world. "Since I was a little girl," Martha says, "I always loved being outside. I grew up in the suburbs and longed to be in the woods. Until I could move away to a wilder place, I spent a lot of time in my backyard studying caterpillars, moths, working in our vegetable garden, and trying to tell a grackle from a starling. When I was twenty-two, I moved to Eugene, Oregon, and have lived in the Pacific Northwest ever since. I lived in cities so I could earn a living, but every chance I got I was on a trail or on my paddleboard. Mostly on trails, though, hiking or running."

She ran for miles on the dirt trails of Seward Park, where, she tells me, the oldest trees in Seattle reside. She loved Vinyasa yoga, "especially the 6 a.m. class." She loved "hiking my ass off, especially with views of Mt. Rainier," and backpacking every summer all over Washington, especially the Cascades, the Olympic mountains, and Upper Lena Lake, where she camped with her son. She was also an avid paddleboarder. She would "put in" at Lakewood Marina and paddle to the I-90 bridge. From 2020-2023 she paddled 2-3 times a week in the summer, but got out there every month of the year, "even when it was frosty and cold and windy," she tells me. "I loved it!"

Martha is also a passionate birdwatcher. Birdwatching, she tells me, "is the thing that makes me happiest after poetry." She is a certified master birder, and she learned to bird *by ear* in a course she took at the University of Oregon. She studied plant taxonomy in her undergraduate days at Grinnell, and "learned every plant in Iowa, just about," she says. "I was an English major, but stopped taking English classes and took mostly biology classes my junior and senior years—organic evolution, marine biology, and other stuff. My taxonomy prof wanted me to get a second BA in Biology and become a research scientist. I took basic chemistry at a community college and got an A, but there was no way I was gonna pass organic chemistry or cell bio." It was when she took a chemistry course at Portland State that she saw they were offering a poetry writing class. "Once I got into the poetry class, well, so long chemistry," she says. "I think I was much happier as an English instructor, teaching creative nonfiction, poetry, and essay writing, than I ever would have been as a researcher, though I continued to learn the plant names in Oregon and Washington, and then I learned the mushrooms…"

Since the onset of her illness, Martha watches birds from her front yard, "or my husband pushes me in a wheelchair around Seward Park," she says, "where we watch for bald eagles, coots, crows, song sparrows, and our favorite: the red-breasted nuthatch, who has a song that sounds like *rhet rhet rhet*." She still loves looking at clouds, and "seeing Saturn rise after dark, especially next to a full moon, seeing Cassiopeia above my head, the giant *W* in the northeastern sky right now."

I think Martha would agree that poetry has space for everything that she has loved and continues to love. Birds and constellations, hikes within view of Mt. Rainier, mothering, teaching, and spending time with her life partner, who has supported her writing and teaching career, as did her parents, who were her biggest fans.

"Poetry gave me a way to share with readers about the natural world, sausages, the names of Oklahoma towns, ladybugs, getting kicked by a fetus, and everything else that awed and inspired me," she says. It is this sense of awe that Martha brings to every poem and every subject, even the painful ones, even the devastating ones. Catastrophe does not diminish her awe. In one poem, she states "that the amount of misery is equal to or greater than the number of eggs / a termite queen will lay in a lifetime—165 million."

Although only *Terminal Surreal* was written since Martha's diagnosis, it is uncanny that she writes poems about climate change, its calamitous impact on the world she loves, and about animals in pain. "The Caspians nesting / on a very hot roof. What the conservation scientist said: *They confuse the dust from the cement plant // with beach.*" Many of these new poems address illness and mortality, for which the ecology poems have served as prelude, or allegory. "I wrote a book of poems about having ALS while I could still write," she tells me. She also made it a goal to finish every one of her unfinished poems. "I had hundreds, and I'm almost done," she says.

In many of the recent poems, she often considers aftermath, for instance, what comes after blooming. She weighs darkness, inventorying it rather than caving to it: "half of every day in darkness most of the cosmos most / of a forest most of the ocean the corridors / that lead to more corridors … the ink from squid / the eggs from a sturgeon Australia's rarest // opals the bear and the panther the ink in the pen on the page … crows and ravens / a window where no one's home charred trees / brushfire's aftermath." Martha still and always will turn to the natural world for her litanies, her metaphors. "When This Boat My Body // pulls into the harbor, the lichens say luck, say love, / sing a funeral song I thought I knew / but don't, still don't." In the same poem, she gives us a line that will live with me always: "It's impossible to know how to punctuate dusk, conjugate / a cormorant."

There are things beyond language's capacity to *mean,* but what Martha does with that is to continue to walk into the shadows. Rather than cataloging what is broken, she lists what is *un*broken. "What's held together / despite the physics of entropy. A bouquet // of oxeye daisies, heal-all, purple clover. This daughter / sipping Coke Starlight. The path to the upper house, / the swing that renders her dizzy … Cygnus on her flight across the summer sky. Deneb, / its 1,900-year-old light, its diameter 135 times // the size of the sun. So much stays whole." It strikes me, as I read her, that her lack of cynicism, and concurrent lack of sentimentality, is directly linked to her love of biology and taxonomy. In a poem called "Poetry," she advises that we "Flourish like a leaf leafing / like a Kentucky spring, like the network in a stem…" She asks us to consider the "cathedrality of mountains" and I do, because I have read her, and consequently, I trust her.

"Everything Ends," she writes, "but so what." I'm not sure if she's speaking to herself or us when she cautions us against pessimism. "Because days spent in a tender mess / are unrecoverable. Naked and floodlit, cocooned // in the opposite of random, we remind ourselves / of the importance of seaweed and seasons, // of each and every bacteria, how we're more / microbe than human. If everything ends, // why are you sharpening your sorrow, / running to catch the discomfort." I take note that there are no question marks here. Her questions are declarative, and irrefutable.

There is a nearly unimaginable generosity in Martha's willingness to allow us to accompany her into the nuanced tenderness of her response to her diagnosis— "I thought it would be like a thumb coming down / on a spider's body, but it was not"—and to her symptoms, "… ahhh, what was this thing with my voice, why was it getting harder / to swallow and speak? When I googled, I found hideous things. / To lightly fly away, like a rosy maple moth. Slowly, // but not too slow. To flutter in the key of yellow and pink, / without coughing or wheezing, / without a bat-like resistance." And she is still noticing; maybe now more than ever, that great brain is working overtime, as when she learns that "… *Catastrophically* // is an anagram of *amyotrophic lateral sclerosis.*"

Like many of us who find ourselves up against the wall of mortality and madness, Martha turns to Keats, but in "I didn't understand Keats's 'Ode to a Nightingale,'" it's a mad and mortal romp, and she knows she's earned it. "Some lady on YouTube / said Keats is drunk at this point in the poem, but my take is he's contemplating / suicide—a bubbly cocktail to snuff himself out because let's face it: being tubercular / is worse than ALS: he shook and groaned with pain, whereas all I'm dealing with / is The *weariness*, a tad of *fret* … *Embalmed darkness*, which reminds me I need to figure out / who's doing my cremation …" My god, who could get away with this but Martha Silano? And yet, at the end, a turn. Maybe she lets Keats off the hook. "Something's buried deep, though hopefully / the music never flees, the music that is poetry."

I believe the last poem she wrote for this collection is a sequence of five linked American Sonnets which she calls "Self-Elegies." It is good to know she is still at it, even at midnight when she reads "a book about microbes and fungi, how these critters / find a way into us, never leave. It's the never-leaving part / I like." As I read Martha's poems, I realize I am reading a life more massive than Mt. Rainier, more proliferative than eagles doing a "locked-talons flip-glide over the lake," more consequential than poems. Poems are poems, not lives, which Martha compares to "alpine snow that seems it will never melt," but they do extend our purview, court the future, contain spinning helixes of our DNA. I am grateful to Henry Israeli and Saturnalia books, and of course, to Martha herself, that we have access to these Marthas, these iterations of everything she reveled in and felt, what she calls, in one of the sonnets, "all these freaking feelings," her wisdom, and her urgent love.

NEW POEMS

THE BLOOMING

had given way to what comes after. What comes after.
The huckleberries that were plump and sweet
now dry on the tongue. I noticed the leaves

were turning red, were red. A hike on a dry, rocky trail
I asked you about Teddy, whether the fall to his death
was an accident, to remind me

how it happened. *He went up a ridge. They found his body
three hundred feet below.* I let that fact
hang in the air.

Do you think he might have found out the day before
he was terminal? I mean, he was so fit, so agile.
Teddy would be the last person I'd expect…

but *no*, he said, *Teddy wasn't that kind of a guy,
to make his friends go looking for him.*
What comes after.

We calculate the time we have left, assuming it's a die-of-old-age
situation. But Teddy. He was our age. Sitting
with that knowing we might not have

thirty years. Pretty much everything
but the asters had gone to seed.
A few lupine blooms,

a shock of fireweed along a granite ridge. I hated
passing under the powerlines, buzzing
as if alive.

I WAS TRYING TO WEIGH DARKNESS

I was trying to weigh darkness how much does darkness weigh
why is my daughter afraid of the dark why was I in my 30s
and 40s afraid of the dark

half of every day in darkness most of the cosmos most
of a forest most of the ocean the corridors
that lead to more corridors

the lover and the corpse what isn't green or yellow or red
what isn't a rainbow a cloud or the moon
when it's reflecting sunlight

what isn't the blue above is ominous unknown
our eyes unable our pupils the ink from squid
the eggs from a sturgeon Australia's rarest

opals the bear and the panther the ink in the pen on the page
a phone when it's not in use the little cocktail dress
the evening gown the tuxedo

a way to be fancy a way to be goth crows and ravens
a window where no one's home charred trees
brushfire's aftermath

WHY I'D LIKE TO MEET MY MAKER

Because She will tell me whether Keebaek's telling the truth
about his absence (suicidal friend, cat with an abscess, missed bus);

because we can have ourselves a chat about gravity, lusty pull
coalescing particles into stars, planets, us. Maybe I'm nosey,

overly forward, but I will be wanting answers about not only
Stonehenge and Roswell but unspeakable evil. As for the yellow-

spotted millipede, I will commend Her for peristaltic motion,
somites and diplosomites, on pest-deterring hydrocyanic acid.

Because She will share Her thoughts on cruelty, on the abuses
of power. While She's nodding you're welcome, providing me

with sensible answers, I will be thanking Her for chartreuse
and sienna, for salmonberry blossoms and gazelles, the rising

warmth of cinnamon rolls, the rising trill of a purple finch,
but I will also be asking how it feels to be held accountable,

to have Abraham asking *Will you really sweep away the righteous
with the wicked?* And speaking of sweeping away, I will be pointed

about funnels and twisters, the magnetic separation of isotopes,
I mean, uranium enrichment. How did you feel about that explosion

on July 16, 1945, I will ask, the one a blind girl saw from 120 miles away,
or had you turned your back long ago on the Valles Caldera,

the Jemez Mountains, that rusty, rouge-y rhyolite? Because I will listen with an open mind, but I will also likely be shaking my head, pointing

to the charred bodies filling the streets of Nagasaki and Hiroshima, at the 528 children who perished in the Pakistani floods.

WHAT IS TOO MUCH

wanting. When is it too much. Like one too many Dark
and Stormies. To avoid the question, I learned to list,
learned to live underground like an insect

raking the soil, like a grizzly in a cave, a place to slow
my heartbeat, down to nineteen from eighty-four.
If you want

to become full, let yourself be empty, said Lao-Tzu. A diving beetle
skating on a pond. If you want to become full,
grow notational legs like little oars.

Being given everything is like the nest that doesn't fall,
is like not finding the broken blue-green egg.
Not displaying yourself,

you're the opposite of a seminar on water, more a research paper
on the hermit thrush. When is it too much wanting,
too much leaning on your tripod gait,

your hoarfrost, your crepuscular. You thought the goal was wings,
didn't know the most evolved
aspire to winglessness.

WHEN THIS BOAT MY BODY

pulls into the harbor, the lichens say luck, say love,
sing a funereal song I thought I knew
but don't, still don't.

When this boat my body meanders into the calm,
the bare willows do not shake or turn
but say with their buds

the woods are filled with the promise of robins,
with crossbills grasping the ends of branches
till the branches bow down.

When I enter the harbor, a loon waves its foot
so I wave my foot back, do a mollusk dance,
write a poem in the seaweedy sand.

It's impossible to know how to punctuate dusk, conjugate
a cormorant. When I let my sails down,
a harbor seal waves from the waves.

I have lived too long with a rudder that refuses to steer
except toward the line from an old song: *Dance
to your daddy, to your mummy sing.*

POSTPARTUM PSYCHOSIS

Sometimes I say I was saved. Sometimes I say
it was the starlings, the ones that took over

the birdhouse in the pear tree (it had sat empty
for years). My grandfather built it from cedar,

painted it white. Empty. The paint peeling,
'til one spring it erupted with squawking.

Sometimes I say I was brought to slaughter,
but really that was an ambulance on its way

to a locked ward. Did I ever share how I sipped
muddy water from a trough? But that was just

the Ativan, Risperidone, Wellbutrin, Celexa,
Lithium. Honey, that was just the nurse

who brought me a breast pump, yelled at me
for saying the French toast was made from shit.

Not so high above us, iridescence. Not so far away
the busiest of birdbaths. My father called it a commune.

My mother looked away. When we love something,
we say we're a pig in mud. When we're out of our minds,

we say we're coo-coo for Cocoa Puffs. When I was an insect
banging against the rafters, when I believed I could fly,

they got out the giant fly swatter. Sometimes I say
I lost my mind. The doctors called it bipolar disorder,

what my shrink referred to as waking nightmares.
I thought I saw my father in the hallway,

telling me the starlings were immoral for shacking up
with the grackles. My mother said all I needed to do

was climb to the top of a mountain. Squeak, squeak
said the starlings. Snort said the pig. It took a year

to climb out of that pen, a year to manage a walk downstairs
to the basement. Someone said my brain was on fire,

that a small spark morphed to a blaze. All I needed
was to turn on the hose, dampen the flames.

BLESSED ARE THEY THAT MOURN

O loving God
O Christ the redeemer
O Jesus with hands in the air
or under a robe

We can create almost anything
Flame with bowl
Good shepherd with staff
Finito Angel

We can rod
We can green pasture
We can valley and table

Sleep on sweet mother and wife
Take thy rest
God called thee home
He thought it best

Through kind more difficult miss
Through never-dies grassmarker

Madonna with dove
Praying Madonna
Madonna with hand on heart

God saw you getting tired
Your text here
18 characters per line
Choose options
starting at $632.00

The face and voice of Pinebrook Golf
By wisdom a house is built
God's love personalized
in 3-5 days

May the glow may life
May the life
To hold better
the withered and decayed

AND YET IT MOVES

~ *Galileo Galilei*

Imagine Galileo, grinding lenses to concavity,
curvature, to causing incoming light
to refract.

Guesswork. Tinkering. Reconfiguring
the glass till he got it to sixty power.
Military uses, of course. Eyeing

the Tower of St. Giustina from thirty miles away,
ships that wouldn't be visible for two hours.
Soon he aimed it at the moon,

discovered ridges, craters, nothing close to smooth.
The surface as spotted as the tail of a peacock,
he wrote, *a crackled and wavy glass vase.*

He sketched our blemished satellite, then studied Jupiter,
its four 'stars' that seemed to be orbiting
the Jovian world.

Philosophers, clergymen, and popes questioned what he was seeing,
insisted the lenses must be faulty, that no way
could Copernicus be right,

no way could the sun be the center, not the Earth.
An anti-Galileo society formed even before
he shared the sun was imperfect too,

blemished with spots. A trial ensued, and the Starry Messenger—
refusing to recount, refusing to cave to those who insisted
if the Earth revolved, it was moved

by angels because *the Earth has no limbs
or muscles ...does not move*—
was put under house arrest.

WHAT ISN'T BROKEN

> ~ *after Dorianne Laux*

The fog-tinged sky. The slatted sunporch floor. My mother's brooch
in the shape of a heart, its shattered seashells spray-painted gold.
Unbroken the deep blue *Brodiaea*, its thin stems

waving in the meadow below the apple tree I want to call unbroken,
though its trunk is split near the top. An antler dangling
from a rusted pulley. Early spring's trestled snap peas,

the many-branched Douglas fir beside what was once a listing barn.
Decades ago, the kernels of corn I instructed my son to drop
into small, dark holes. Each blackberry

foraged from the brambles near a van we no longer own.
The spiderweb in the sword fern. Did one of my ribs
shatter? Did my little brother crack it

when he pushed me out of bed? I couldn't inhale without sharp pain,
told my mother (her silence: entire). What's held together
despite the physics of entropy. A bouquet

of oxeye daisies, heal-all, purple clover. This daughter
sipping Coke Starlight. The path to the upper house,
the swing that renders her dizzy.

Vega, Altair, and Sadr. The entire swan on a moonless night,
Cygnus on her flight across the summer sky. Deneb,
its 1,900-year-old light, its diameter 135 times

the size of the sun. So much stays whole. Gravity keeping books
and pens on a table, the sun and moon where they need to be,
two bumble bees whining at the window.

All of it complete, including the now-and-then call of a flycatcher:
ee-oo-eet? All of it, including my heart, this beating heart,
so not my mother's, especially those final days

when her son took over, took her over. My heart a sturdy cup,
so unlike the cereal bowls and dinner plates,
lacking a single chip.

WHAT I WISHED FOR

Me, as a flag iris. A.k.a., wild.

Me, spending a year with my father's yellowing files, his yellowing eyes.

Me, in a bog.

Me, with some of me gone.

Me, beside *Coreopsis,* beside clouds.

The me of remember, of my uncle's clarinet, notes coasting toward Bleeding Hearts.

Me, passing from now to between, from refusing needlework
to welcoming the electricity of the sentence, homonyms, and rhyme.

Me, which has no synonym.

Me, like a weevil in the skunk vine.

Me, distantly, like a magnificent frigate bird high above a pier.

Me, always on the verge of reappearing with the answer: the great egress.

Oh, to be planting luster. Oh, to be weeding the caveats. Removing
each rusty ache.

To bore into a pond, break to the surface with a hurray fish.

My wishes like a promised sandbox I made good on. Made good on,
then smothered with a bed of haricot-verts.

What I wished for was to be more like the blue daze of napping
in the middle of the day, the Johnny-Go-to-Bed-at-Noon.

I wished for a lifetime of Saturdays, though Mondays were my secret love.

Me, with seaweed hair.

For an abundance of bougainvillea, one small handful of tasks.

For departure's opposite, an undying slice, not too salty, not too robust.

THE WEEDS

She's always getting into the goddam weeds.
Never on the periphery.
Never on the berm.
Loves to commune with the bulrush and the reeds.
Psssshing out rails and grebes.
Once she said she spotted a water thrush, native to New Orleans. A migrant, she said.
In them weeds again? her grandma would ask.
In them weeds where there might be a frog to befriend.
A being who might understand her preference for pickerel weed.
For the minutiae in the mallow, the particulars in the panicles.
For each specific spikelet, every willow and cattail nuance.
What's up with her and her goddamn weeds.
Why's she always out there in her waders, marveling at marsh hawks?
Who told her to peek under rocks, stand amongst the bulrush, waiting for a bittern to appear?
Why can't she resist the detritus of the details, the intricacies of estuaries?
Wetland-shwetland: what the heck. So done with her, her mudflat search for truth.

SONG

Goes like this: a bill is what you pay,
what you owe. To cleave is stick together /

fall apart. The bridge goes clip, clip, clip
(to fasten, to detach), the dike prevents

the flood, is the ditch where the flood
will come to rest. A melody's dollop

can be large or small; a refrain's dust
accumulates, is swept away with a cloth.

Goes like holding fast / scuttling away,
stuck or in a rush; goes like that song

I can't remember, though the worm's
in my ear like a bolted door on the run.

The singer? Bound, but not right now
while she does her soldering. Is a song,

is a longing, ever finished as in done,
as in all washed up? What's left

and what remains? Gone to seed
or hell, that house of the rising sun,

weakened or having succeeded,
go figure. Is it one-of-a-kind or a copy,

asked the model musician. Do screens
reveal or conceal? Is Rock-n-Roll

immobile or a shaking, swiveling
disco ball? (Cleave with me, baby.

Cleave me.) When the tape is spliced
is it joined or wrenched apart?

Let me throw this out: my journey
was a stumble, my endurance

wore me out. I did not wear it well.
I wound up ending at the start.

WHEN I BEGAN TO DIG

this is what I found: from the Latin, *vertere,*
to turn, from the Lithuanian, *versti,* to overturn,

from the Sanskrit, *vartate,* he turns. *Vers, fers:*
turning, turning and bending, having planted

a length of beans or corn, having reached a furrow's
end. Like a plowman, *versing,* this breaking up

of sod, this fashioning into tidy rows, helping the singers
recall their lines. When the need to memorize

disappeared, *verse* remained like the typewriter keys
spelling QWERTY, slowing the typist down. When I began

to dig, I found *turn, turn back, be turned, convert, transform,
be changed.* From *wert:* to wind, its cognate *weard*

(turned toward). When I began to dig I unearthed
wyrd (destiny, fate), found *what befalls one,* reached

down, pulled up *Turn! Turn! Turn!* A Pete Seeger tune,
a psalm. From Slovenia to Wales, from Greece

to Ireland: *turn, turn, stir, ladle, become.* This *verse,*
this *versus,* likened to conversion, a breather,

a fresh start. Poet, like a plowman in a field
with his furrowed words, looking for a good excuse

to put up his brow, wipe his feet, reward herself
for making it this far. When I dug I found porridge,

bread (barley and rye), lentils, peas, eggs. Not much
meat. Small amount of vegetables and fruit. I found

oats; I found ale. What the digging revealed
was a single word meaning destiny *and* clean

slate, befalling fate yoked to the notion of free will.
To translate, become someone or something else.

In that plowman's act, an apparent contradiction
as great as any Yin and Yang, koan-like conundrum,

that when we don binoculars to study a common
word, English sparrow of the lexicon, we find the link

between poetry and confrontations large and small—
tournaments, showdowns, battles—between a book

of poems, and Sunday's nail-biting match-up
between the Seahawks and the Panthers. *Versus*,

a word connecting whatever force, power, or god
handed Marshawn Lynch his strength, his knack

for eluding the tackle, his Shakespearean grace,
and the task of the poet: to bury the weeds;

to disembalm the knotted, entwining roots,
the richest loam. To make, of the oldest question,

a song: are we free or are we not?

THE VITAL QUESTION

has something to do with a close up of a human cell
beads and strings   an exquisite necklace

with cutting away the finesse   keeping the mornings
losing the way past dusk   don't live your life in a maybe kind of way

my father said   tell me how and why and I will tell you
what I've been told like an egg that doesn't know

its forthcoming wing   God's mouth is full of the bluest kind
of mystery solved   that a flame has a shadow   that there is no scale

to weigh the sky   no pushpins in the hypothermal vents
no Post-its for the flashpoints   no scalpelling the wonder

no taking a gloved hand   reaching into the ocean   to find the source
no pointing to the exact place where it all began

POETRY,

they said. Focus like a plank of wood stays focused
on the plank it rubs against, the nails,
on the warping as they age. Stay

creative. Like others, create. Flourish like a leaf leafing,
like a Kentucky spring, like the network in a stem.
Let your brain be French or Guyanese, create

un-dreading routines. In place of late trains, place mountains
and Ferris wheels in your dreams. Motivational quotes,
like *Look as carefully at yourself*

as you do the sun. Cultivate the unexpected like cultivating
plums. Become the uncommon prune of the ages.
Find a new word for *walls*. Focus

on Plank's constant, on the quark known as *charm*.
Try having your best lifetime, though a Guinness
is fine, a cocktail with a hibiscus base.

Be the antidote and the anecdote. Force books and windfall apples
onto your besties, six-foot clams and fossils of camels from here
to Spokane. Reverse adversity while confronting arthritis

of the mind. Enough is not always enough. Call it
an independence growing less ominous
across the Midwest, something akin

to the Saint Louis Arch. Especially in the morning,
listen to pigeons and scientists. Endurance
is within your gasp. Outside Austin,

pop your lines, make them go feather, un-rust.
Let your noggin weirden: it helps. Each of us,
like an apron or an albatross,

has a back and front. X out judgment. Your theater
is a doorway: improve on what can be improved,
on a little strategic wandering

beyond the recipe. Limit the part of you that doesn't want
to be a child. Unrigid your flagpole. Sharp can be bad
but also works, the zeitgeist in your kombucha.

Mine non-operatic projects. Be the movie that ends
with a bright black beetle. Don't let social media
tailor your musings, though let it if it will.

Except when you're not, be a language economist. Let passion
be your business, 9 to 9. Your reward? Handstands,
an open-ended stylus, singing by the pound.

ARS POETICA

Some say Deception Pass is the perfect climate
for a determined violinist, a Dali devotee.

Some say it's important to block the view
of the pier, but then there's the lapping

of invisible pilings smothered in barnacles,
sturdy artistes of the sea with their thermoses

of port, bivalves who know when to take
the phone off the hook, put the VHS on pause,

unplug the vacuum and the strobe.
Pollock slept most days until early afternoon,

resisted dripping, drizzling, or splashing till
he'd fired off 10,000 missives, his wife

encircling his shuffling feet like a nest
of tongue-flicking vipers. Some say a mountain

is like a roasting chicken, that bump at the top
where the wings fan out, indication the masterpiece

has reached 160 degrees, is ready for the platter.
Some say it's better to skip the wallowing,

the two poached eggs, get right down to the whisky
and the grief, to the gold nugget god-awful cellar

of the self. Some say break for lunch, some say
break only when the raccoons have finished

their wrestle in the desiccated, isopod-laden
kelpweed. Some say never begin or end

on a Friday, never fly-away but always a kerchief.
Some say no life vest, no moorage, no mast.

I SOLD MY PREDICATES,

gave away my adjectival clauses. Took a trip to the city of split up and plead. When I tried to locate my mother, I couldn't hit the target so I relocated. It was like what they say about the geologic curl, all the chert and basalt deciding it needed a Brazilian blow-out. I knew I should go visit Brianne or Darcy, but I just couldn't bring myself to anywhere but a saloon on the last cobblestone street in Seattle. Effort was the last thing on my mind. Foremost was the fact Jackson Pollock slept until midday, a deer tick riding a five-point buck into splattered stardom. I should have been a sludge cricket, a slender egg, Ophelia's trophy wife. We all have our billion garden bulls, our fruitions stuck in God's ditch, but I wanted my emergency window to unhinge, my thought ambulance to screech to a haute. We all have our gourd days and bat days, but I hate it when my violets walk out. And that dead dog's paw, entombed in Glad Wrap, placed beside the meat paddies in the freezer. I don't think I'd understood, until then, grief. Not one optimistic fleece left in your herd of sheep. I kept the moon, one poem, three nephews. What I couldn't depose of, I shook off.

THE BALD EAGLES OF SEWARD PARK

always surprise me, always make me
believe trying to fix a mistake is worth it.
Case in point: DDT, an insecticide used to eradicate

diseases like malaria and typhus.
Eradicating mosquitoes because, well,
first and foremost: the health and safety of people.

God forbid a human should've known
how this chemical would weaken the eggshells of eagles,
inching down the number in the lower 48 from 100,000 to

just 417. Yes, they harass ospreys, steal their prey, so it
kinda makes sense Ben Franklin said *He does not get his
Living honestly,* preferred, for our national bird, the wild turkey, but

mating for life – what's not to like? Google *Eagles and DDT*, find
NO adverse effects on humans, domestic animals, or wildlife – really?
Opinions graciously accepted. Free speech, I guess, which proliferates,

propagates like these eagles, where on a good day I
question how there could be so much chattering and pealing,
roosting and gliding. That there would be so many juveniles

soaring over the water, diving down to nab a perch.
Talon-grabbing and tumbling while mating. Cloacal kissing.
Utterly promising, isn't it? A success story! What was alarming

very much less dire now. That we banned it.
Wailed and moaned *no, no, no*. That the EPA prevented
X-ing out a regal raptor that's been around a million years, its

(yowzers) reptilian past. Stopped the slide from abundantly robust to
zero. That we might restore tall grass prairies, save the bees that feed us.

THERE'S SO MUCH TO ADMIRE

about ammonites, I don't know where to begin.
Like this place called Kremmling, Colorado,
where so many died

it's like a graveyard. It's mostly a theory, but some believe
they were spawning under a full moon
when the sea suddenly warmed,

became acidic, and/or lost all its oxygen, or else they died
because there were no offspring, and ammonites
eat their young.

Or that the sky darkened when an asteroid crashed into Yucatan,
which pretty much halted photosynthesis, so bacteria
dominated the seas, as it had

for millions of years before. This one paleontologist on *YouTube*
said "they retain their whole life history in their shells."
I bet we do the same. I bet some creature,

millennia from now, will run tests on our bones, analyzing
the carbon and oxygen isotopes, calculate the acidity
of our oceans, the amount of carbon

in our atmosphere right before the equivalent
of a great spawning extravaganza—
the tides high, the moon's light

forging a glittery path across the dark waves
of Exxon-Mobile, Conoco and Standard Oil.
Named by Pliny the Elder after Ammon,

an Egyptian god who sported a ram's horn, early collectors
called them *snake stones*, sold them
for their curative powers.

The Blackfeet, noting their resemblance to buffalo,
used them in ceremonies before hunts.
In Germany, the cure for a dry cow:

place a *curie* in the milking pail, while in Rome tucking one
under one's pillow was said to produce
prophetic dreams. Louis Agassiz,

a pal of Cuvier, lecturing on the coiling and uncoiling
of their shells, compared their twisted forms
to the writhing contortions

of a death struggle. Others referred to them as *bizarre forms*
having the *appearance of abnormality*. We now know
they were adapting to their environment,

evolving when random mutations proved beneficial, filling
more and more niches until there were 10,000-plus
species, and 30 body types, including *Parapuzosia*,

six feet in diameter. Some resemble hair pins, pointy tipped
carrots. Many retained a spiraling form. If you visit
Kremmling, the first things you'll come upon

are a Subway and a Kum & Go. We've been around for 300,000 years,
but the ammonites hung on for 350 million. They thrived
in methane seeps, a toxic gas that kills us,

adapted to catastrophe until they no longer could, until a sudden
influx of carbon wiped them out. An influx less sudden
than the one we face.

THE SIGNS WERE CLEAR

at the botanical garden where hot irises pulsed
with hormones, where my daughter asked, *won't you
take me down to fuchsia town?* Where I let nature do the heavy lusting,

where trying to read the map, we settled
into our senses. After she dropped her iPhone in the heliotrope,
after macerating our raw emotions, we declared our import impermeable,

our inlets unlettable. Poetry became a kind of piety,
a lien on our longings, its bringing a kind of brining, each line—
No Snapchatting Your Gentians!—a dogged lessening as verse morphed

to virtue. *You're kissing me!* teased
the resolute macaw as we strolled past the barricaded barracudas,
stopping only for a hot cup of repose, halcyon with a twist, our horrors

morphing to hammocks, our fears a giant neon hibiscus.
No longer confined to the banks, we danced like errant electron,
asking a penny for your peony? A twenty for your beach verbena?

No matter how many todays ran by like rodents, we'd be,
if not well, at least wielding, not holed up but howled up, hoped up,
raising our violent violets to a trajectory of sob-stopping nasturtiums,

would carry our griefcases to the end
of a short pier, blow out the rushed and breathe in the hushed,
catch a *wowie-wowie-wooo-weeeeee* wave. I signed my name *Meatball,*

Masthead, Mashers, anyone but who I'd been,
as I watched our difficults dull, our sufferings suffuse
with spatterdock, no one and nothing able to blue our minds,

our burrs morphing to birds. You can tittle
like a turtle, I assured. Stop maudling and start moving ever closer
to the lyric hills; trade your stigmata and hairshirt for avocets and stilts.

WHEN WISPY CLOUDS DRIFT THROUGH SPARSELY WOODED MOUNTAINS

When the contours of mountains resemble coliseums.
Cathedrality of mountains.
Relief of roadlessness.

That there are lakes impossible to reach by car.
That from this window just behind the wing, 20F,
there are no signs of life.

Once I packed a bag with cheddar goldfish.
Once my son threw up before we even boarded the plane.

Cracks and fissures, cuneiform of rock. Backbones and capillaries,
the snaking green edged with bluffs (long-ago ocean?).

He will turn eighteen next week.

Brain-like contours – cerebral cortex or cerebellum?
Contours thin like the veins of leaves, fronds of a sword fern, feet of a coot.
Time passed like a silent rail in the reeds.

The folds Egyptian, mummies reposed in their tombs.
Like an alligator's enormous tail, though lacking snout and teeth.

Once I sang *La crocodile il est malade, il est malade a Singapour.*
All those years, I thought I was singing *sangue a peu* – a little blood.

Clouds less cumulus, more cumulonimbus.
Towns scattered with houses like paint chips.

From the ground he would wave to the passengers in the sky: *Bye-bye, babies!*

Claw-like hills, afghan of cloud not like fresh snow but snow a few days old,
the occasional indentation where a foot or tire met asphalt.

The crocodile is sick. A little mercy, a little blood.
Between fluffy swirls, black holes.

When the binky and the sippy cup.
When the diaper bag and the teething ring.
Cottoned from above
like first tracks on Lynx Pass,
a pristine path through aspen, lodgepole, spruce.

DASHING

What's funny is my son calling me
an hour into his *Door Dash* shift:
*Mom, I'm having a bit
of an emergency.*

I'm thinking rear-ended, injured, totaled the car.
*The light turned green and someone jumped
in front of me, so now there's milkshake
all over the passenger floor.*

Funny because my son is still alive, because the emergency
turned out to be whipped cream, four long-stemmed
maraschinos, the red not of blood,
the emergency solved

with a bucket and sponge. What's funny is my healthy son
hosing down the floor mat, handing a solicitor a twenty
for a measure to make Medicare for all,
asking *so what's it like*

going door to door as the sticky sweetness
floats toward the street. What's funny
is I'm healthy too—nothing broken,
nothing a little ibuprofen

and yoga won't cure. So often I forget my lines,
fall in and out of line, want to fall to my
Chablis because, as Jack Gilbert says,
the heart in its plenty hammered

by rain and need. And when he writes *the sound of a stone
hitting / a stone in the dark*...I mean, think about that
for a sec: *a stone hitting a stone,*
not in the sun

or under fluorescent tubes, but in some dank place
so opposite of a son coming home with rosy
splatters on his navy-blue shirt,
what could be shards

of catastrophe scrubbed away. The floor mat's dripping
on the side porch railing. *Okay, Ma, I'm Dashing
again.* Waving, slowly backing out,
into the pink-tinged dusk.

THE DOE OUTSIDE OUR BACK DOOR

is chewing with her eyes closed,
spittle dribbling down her chin.

Fearless, her ears two semaphores
signaling calm. Chewing

like a construction worker
holding up a SLOW sign, fur

like mown hay drying in the sun.
My daughter says she must be

a little bit out of her mind,
but so must I, enthralled

by this scruffy ungulate
chewing like a hairdresser

laying down a perm at Hair Today,
Gone Tomorrow, a wash and set

at Curl Up & Dye. Chewing,
by the wild rose and serviceberry,

like she's lounging on a sofa
in the family den, catching up

on the soaps like a sailor
on the fat of a summer afternoon.

AND THE ROAD IS LIKE A CAVE WITH YELLOW WALLS

that are leaves, which I point out to my son,
how beautiful, how beautiful the fog, the fact
that my head isn't pounding like it did all night,
like it has for years, like fertility made me sick,
like losing my fertility made me sick, like I thought
the end of releasing eggs would end my pain,
when instead I strain to delight in two kayakers
bobbing in the whitecaps. If anyone from the American
Cancer Society asks you for a dime, I say to my son,
ask them why don't they ask Tyson, why not
Proctor & Gamble, but really what I'm asking
is why do you have to grow up, why can't you be
that blonde boy sprinkling sand into a kiddy pool
one small blue shovelful at a time, why do I keep
dreaming you're a baby. And the road is a cave,
and we're talking about how easy it is to get enough
protein—a couple cups of legumes and a PBJ,
sharing how I asked his sister, are you sure
you didn't imagine a giant gray moth in the night
singing like a cicada? And the mustard leaves
are a tunnel down the boulevard by the water,
safe for kayakers and muskrats, a few small trout.

IN ANOTHER LIFE

In another life my name was Cocoa Rockledge.
I was sweet but dangerous, my legs thick
with arithmetic, my arms like the birth

of Venus, like a blabbermouth at a house party.
My breath sprawled across a row of peaks,
attuned to the burgeoning melody of schist.

When I was Cocoa Rockledge, each night astounded me
like the climax of an opera by Puccini.
Each morning I'd waken

like a three-sided stem aspiring to be grass.
When I let out my breath, my mouth
was the mouth of the Thames,

my hands two speckled leaves beneath the Whitehall Bridge.
My song was what you wake to
at Gulch Creek campground

in June: *hick-three-beers* (a flycatcher on steroids).
Steadfast and dependable, Cocoa was never
an obedient cow, never raised a sponge

or mop. From her, I learned to never recoil
or constrict. To gather windfall walnuts
from a pile of crumbling bricks.

LAST TRAIN TO PARADISE

My hairdresser my salonist my sweet Mariah drops the f-bomb while mixing my color drops the spatula dabs my forehead to keep the dye from dying on the wall's a strawberry plant both budding and fruiting a pearly everlasting like getting my hair back to a shade of black it's never been I'm a beagle of eavesdropping on the clientele *They met at Walter Payton 1600 on the SAT* a peony that's always pink a lily that never keels over in the pre-rain October near the gated community where they joke about the ice age my darling Mariah explaining how I need to use more product bow my head and shake it to lessen the frizz says she left her man when he told her *Your entire life is a complaint* says when he said it she asked him to say it again *say it so I know I can leave you* the one getting her silvers clipped says there hasn't been a storm like this since 1935 when it took out the Last Train to Paradise & wouldn't we all love to be raising a Line 39 to the gators that live to be a hundred last call for a ride from NYC to the Keys for a blowout a blowjob a blousy hurray for Mariah who tells me she might at 57 be starting a new life

BUYING AND SELLING

I bought shares in deer lilies, in Dave's Killer Bread,
in towns named Evening Shade and Horseshoe Bend.
In the trail to Happy Camp. The song I sing

is urgent like the Salmon River at flood stage, like a boot
that must keep hiking. There must be a rodent
for the Van Gogh in all of us,

a rat not only for my tomcat Taco, but for anyone who needs
a little knapsack of natural. Someone said we were all
created to enter a chasm, to just once crawl into

a hole, fling open the storm cellar, let in the befallen.
Once we let them in, there's no room left
for signs that say *Fuck Biden*,

for Swastikas, though plenty of room for the graves
of the disillusioned. You were a mattress
with springs poking out, but now

you're a wakened prairie—wild bergamot, black-eyed Susan.
When you make a trade, nothing hurts except what happens
under the fluorescent lights of a Whole Foods

when you can't afford a bottle of olive oil, a $4.00 Honey Crisp.
When a star falls, does it really fall? It doesn't really fall.
A stranger picks it up and calls it a miracle,

calls it salt. Whenever I search, it's for the snow shovel of my childhood –
maybe it's still sitting there out by the driveway, waiting for me
to clear the sidewalk on 271 Grove.

When I spot Georgia O'Keeffe hanging out with Claude Monet at the NYSE,
drinking Malbec, not discussing GE but comparing brushes,
comparing skulls, I sell my shares in logic,

in the metaverse, in the world on the screen like a game of Monopoly,
including that gray clothes iron they retired in 2013. Oh and la,
a flightless bird gone extinct. Oh and la, the fig tree

in my neighbor's yard, its two fruitings. Oh, oh, and la,
a song about veins and arteries, which, as you know,
we all have.

THE WHOLE VAGINA EXPERIENCE

When I told my friend Hanita it was not a fun time
to be a mom, that the best I could hope for
was détente, not being told

I'd ruined my daughter's life. When I texted Hanita *she chewed me out*
for enrolling her in gymnastics! It's like PTSD, those goddamn
poxed and toxic coaches,

she texted back *shitty teenage years. It's what they do, their rite of passage.*
It helped, really helped, because lord knows I had my rite of shittage too,
telling my mother she'd fucked us all up,

insisting my siblings and I thrive in spite of their ad heck parenting,
telling her all of us have been shrinking on couches for decades,
checking ourselves into ashrams,

ohm-ing to undo the mess of their pieced-together-with-threats nest.
When she calms down, you should illustrate your birth to her.
The whole vagina experience, which took me back

to the hospital where I still walk the hallways, trying to spur on dilation.
I was at 2 cm, wanting to cry. Instead, I crawled on top
of a giant rubber ball, bounced for an hour.

3 cm. Damn. So I walked some more. Found, on the 5th floor, a red and yellow mangle
of a Deborah Butterfield horse. By 10 pm I'd gotten to 6! Not enough
to start pushing, but by one in the morning I could.

I pushed for over an hour. The midwife got close to my face:
You need to take a deep breath and push harder
than you've ever pushed in your life.

And then she was there. She was crying. She was gray and vernixed and bloody, the cord having been wrapped around her neck. But she was on my chest. They put her there before they cleaned her off, I think, to revive her.

Once she was pink, once it was clear she wasn't going to die, one of the two nurses named Sharon bathed her, brought her back to me, so I could hold her, so I could nurse her, so I could rest.

NOW WE COME TO TICKS AND TOCKS

Totally giddy and grinning as I recall the fox we happened upon,
its eyes the curious eyes of a toddler.
That night a full moon

like a wheel of brie. We were always playing The Garden Game,
my daughter and I, which I'd picked up for a dollar
at Goodwill. Entertained by cards

that said we'd forgotten to mulch, to nourish the humus,
which of course we pronounced *hummus*,
she being a vegan and all.

But now she's fifteen, another word for sulky, disgusted,
annoyed, as in *you really should consider
the application of eyeliner*. The moon

told me I was almost fifty-nine. What I told it was how
it would never be a place where arugula seeds
would grow, but by then it was morning,

the moon on the other side of the world, the clouds and wind
friends we like to gossip with, all the while thinking
she's that fox, not as in *she's such a fox,*

more in the way the fox stayed close, kept going in
and out of sight, never getting within thirty feet.
We are wasting precious time,

Miss Everett used to say. Well, sure, honey,
isn't that the human condition?
Waddling through time

like the duck my daughter turned me into? We christened the fox
Mr. Fox, and she told me *Fox-n-Sox* freaked her out,
scrambled her brain with the chicks and bricks,

with the *quick trick chick stack*, made her feel like a slug
in salt. Then she let me spin again, and I told her
I'd always love foxes.

POEM FOR MY DAUGHTER ON HER 18TH BIRTHDAY

Something about look at me,
don't look at me. Something about
the afternoons, to be loved all afternoon?

We were in a hurry to find each new leaf
along the road to Tay's house, for *signs of spring,
Mama!* Purple crocuses, the thin white stripes on each

green stem. In a hurry, running late,
before my mother went down, down, down
into her grave. You wrote a poem called "Singing Birds":

*chirp, chirp, chirp all the birds sing
at 8 am sharp, just like a robin's beak.* A kind of pain,
a kind of hello/goodbye, a dark and deep tulip, Queen of the Night.

A kind of walk you take what feels
like every day when *all the birds are very happy,*
when nothing has flown, when the sun isn't saying *goodbye,*

goodbye as it goes away, though maybe
that kind of ashamed. We studied each green thing,
found, beneath brown leaves, the moss rejuvenating.

Nothing and no one was saying sorry.
Maybe something was wrong but I didn't
notice. You were two and four and six and eight,

sixteen. The sun set, the birds went quiet,
while your brain kept singing its song of why
is it not okay to be myself, why must I measure myself

against the judgment of others?
But I didn't know. I led you to Tay's, past
the maple that split in a storm, had to be chopped down.

THE PRECISE MODE OF FAILURE COULD NOT BE REPLICATED,

which was another way of saying
I'd done it again (shame, shame)—

had not kept the daughter
from whining, had let the son

spend hours playing Overwatch,
had chosen the incorrect knife

to slice the green tomato, forgot
to pour the melted butter into the batter,

the salt into the dough. How many tests,
how much review, and still the pre-

detection of the error impossible,
anticipation of the mishap/omission

unpredictable, more impossible
to foretell than guessing where the ants

on the kitchen counter are marching from,
why, of all things, they're suffused

with formic acid. I kept being the state
department, believing the attack

was real when it was not. I kept falling
for the passive voice, the best voice

when you need to leave yourself out.

JUST DON'T THINK ABOUT WATERFALLS

Let's face it: these days it's all about finding a place to pee.
Not only in the woods but in one's car, behind
a 150-year-old cedar tree, a water tank

because I can't make it from the grocery store to the automotive place
without revealing myself somewhere, and where does one go
when the QFC restrooms are locked? A Starbucks

cup, of course. A water bottle now designated for such.
A pot I did piss in before this whole thing began,
because the playground north of the zoo

had no bathrooms. Lots of swings. No toilet.
I taught my daughter to pee in the woods
when she was two.

We were at the Whispering Pines RV Park, the only tenters
in that godforsaken grove of spindly lodgepole pines.
Here, honey, let me show you.

She was an expert by the time she was three. What I want to know
is why I wasn't an expert at three, why did my mother
not share with me the art of dropping trou,

of the concert piss, why didn't she deign to give a name
to the thing between my legs?
The boys had something,

but I had ... what? A placeholder, a no-thing, a non.
When I was seven, I returned from school
and my parents weren't home.

Locked out, I realized I hadn't peed since, when? That morning?
School, Brownies, the mile walk home. I panicked.
How does one pee but not on a toilet?

I didn't know I could pull down my white cotton HealthTex briefs,
squat beside the compost pile, add my signature
to the rotting cantaloupe rinds and corn cobs.

So, yeah, I peed myself, the backside of my uniform
the color of mud. And now I smelled
like that girl who smelled like pee,

whose name I still remember but will not share.
Thank God I taught my daughter
it has a name.

Thank God I have the memory of the three of us driving in my mother's Windstar,
my daughter yelling from her car-seat *Mama,*
my buh-DINA!

In the fifty-odd years I knew her, I never once heard my mother say it: *vuh-JINE-uh.*
Out of which pours blood, spermicidal jelly, KY, sperm, and babies.
Out of which, or close enough, comes pee.

Who's to say I'm not peeing right now, not, as my husband
likes to joke, writing at red lights, but while taking
what Holden Caufield called *a leak.*

FONDEST MEMORIES FROM THE LOCKED WARD

Lots of it was painful like no pain I'd ever felt, like when, sipping licorice tea
in the dreary cafeteria, I approached a group at the next table:
Are you talking about me?

It wasn't so great when I heard my father's voice in the hallway,
or when throughout the night an orderly peeked
into the little window at my door

to make sure I wasn't—what—hanging from a bedsheet? Yet,
for some of it I'm nostalgic, like when my roommate
knew all about postpartum psychosis. She was in,

she said, to get her meds back on track. When I told her what I had,
she was all *Oh, yeah! I know about that! Last time I was here
a woman insisted she was the wife of Moses.*

That's me, I said. Only I believed God told me He was tired, would I mind
taking over? All I had to do was figure out a way to reach Him,
shimmy past the giant manger on the roof (Jesus, Mary,

and Joseph, plus a sheep). That first night, when my body refused
to breathe without great effort, as if I had emphysema,
well, it's lucky our brains evolved to forget

the severity of our discomforts. The next morning, I woke to a blue pill
in the bathroom sink, rushed out to tell my roommate
it had to be a sign. No, she assured me—

she'd just had trouble swallowing, When I insisted it had to mean something,
she laughed: *No, really, it's just my spit-out Prozac.* Thankful
for the orderly who let me check out a razor,

though not before asking if I was having suicidal ideations. But no, and oh,
the pleasure of a bath, my first in weeks. Even at the best hospitals
the nurses yell things like *F*cking shit—you had a baby,*

you're gonna be fine! But during the holidays, I made a star
from drinking straws, a wrapped present
from a miniature milk box.

Fondness for the reward of outside time, checking out the heli pad,
where the direst cases arrived. For the day I turned cartwheels
in the parking lot, dizzy with freedom, with joy.

EAT PREY, LOVE

When an owl is hooting outside your bedroom window do you leave your bed,
strap on your headlamp, search the Douglas fir till you find it?
Owl?   *Owl?* I've been meaning to ask if owls fall in love,
or is it something else. Hoot-n-love? Eat prey, love?

My aloneness weighs less than the footprints of shrews. What's a soulmate, anyhow?
I think it helps if you both would wear a pink feather boa in public, if you know
how to say things like *the vole takes back every hurtful thing it said.*
Oh, the haute couture of the courtship.

Once I took my son on an *Owl Prowl.* Before we set off to stalk
the Great Horned, the leader handed us each what looked
like a scruffy gray mouse. Our job: to poke the pellet
open, scrutinize the bones.

If you're lucky, said the leader, you'll find a jaw or skull. My son
kept asking if we'd see an owl, and when we did
would it turn its head all the way around?
I told him the head trick was lore.

What happens if the mole won't accept your apology? What if you're incapable
of *a la mode*? It seems essential to have silent wings, no whooshing sound.
To know wide wings equals less flapping, less noise.
Do I need to tell you

we hiked two hours, didn't find a single owl? That the trip leader
shined his spotlight on what turned out to be a racoon?
Sometimes a lover's like Polaris, which we did see
that night. Never rising or setting,

dependably shining. And sometimes your mate is like the owl Noctua,
who used to perch on the tail of the Hydra; she's gone now,
along with the mockingbird and the solitary thrush.

I'M NOT SURE WHY I DECIDED

Shelter in Place would equal a book called *The Story of Earth*,
which I read aloud to my husband each night as his breath
begins to louden, lengthen. We are learning our moon
was borne of a colossal collision, aka the Big Thwack,
when a planet named Theia, after the Titan goddess
whose name means *sight*—who birthed the sun and moon
and dawn—wandered into Earth's orbit. "Theia's smooshed,"
I hear myself saying. And then I pause.

                                              And now it's just me
and Theia, her obliteration, though listen: it's Theia, the moon,
and each of us thrown 23 degrees off our axes; really, it's Theia:
some of her escaped into deep space, but her iron is in our core;
she's the one who gave us seasons—each ripening ear of corn,
every trillium and trout lily, the dark cold days and the warmest.

FROM

WHAT THE TRUTH TASTES LIKE

(1998)

THE MAN WHO SLEPT IN MY BED

is somewhere over Oklahoma: Broken Arrow, Shamrock, Marble City.
By now he's bugged the stewardess twice for scotch and soda,

the latest Cowboys/Redskins score. If he isn't asleep,
if he's near a window, he's looking down on Scraper, Nebo,

Joy. And when the honey-roasted peanuts make the rounds:
Bromide, Mustang, Homer. Tries to read and his mind drifts off.

Dreams of open spaces, gray birds with scissor tails,
what it might be like to border Texas, come equipped

with a handle. The captain announces the final score
as the plane glides over Wapanucka, Freedom, Comanche,

Strong, and I'm in my bedroom, eyes glued
to the lower left-hand corner, ten miles west of Friendship,

to the town of Martha. *Why do you have a map of Oklahoma
on your wall?* he asked the night he left. I could sooner explain

Orion, Wheeless, Eagle City. I could sooner explain Love
County, or the South Canadian River. He's somewhere

over Oklahoma circling Crystal, Hollis, Lone Grove.
He doesn't even think of me at Boiling Springs, Ringling,

Purdy, Loco, doesn't know there's an Okay, a Loyal, a Mutual.
Doesn't know we could settle down in Sweet Water, raise a family

in Muse, can't imagine growing old in Sugarville
or camped in the Winding Stair Mountains.

He's somewhere over Oklahoma, not over me.

LADYBUG

When she reaches the end
Of a shoe or a table, she keeps
Walking. If she needs the help of wings,
Wings appear. If she lands on her back,
Her hind legs find the world and turn her
Over. When the wings forget to fold,
They drag like a slip from a scarlet dress.

Where did this one in my kitchen come from?
Did a neighbor, in a fit of aphid rage,
Release a thousand? Is this a sign?
Am I to count the spots?

Time Teller, Child Bringer,
Pursuer of Missing Sheep:
What will be next?
Predacious diving beetles?
Scarabs named Goliath?
Bombardiers that shoot a puff of gas?
Don't uninvited guests bring relatives?

But God's Almighty Cow,
Marienkäfer and Kin to Hen and Dove,
How can I kick you out?

Girls put you on the tips of their fingers.
Where you fly they'll meet a spouse.
Cousin to Whirligig, Sharer of Parts
With the Snouted Weevil, is this the home
Where you thought you'd find
Your children? Whoever sang to you lied.

SWEET RED PEPPERS, SUN-DRIEDS, THE HEARTS OF ARTICHOKES

Pagliacci Pizza wants me.
Lying in bed on a Sunday morning,

I could almost want them back.
The trick, a deliverer said,

is learning to hesitate. Not in the car
or walking to the door, but just

inside, when they're waiting
for change.

Or I could manage a bingo hall,
swirl behind glass at the Lusty Lady.

Once it was a cornfield,
sixteen hours a day in a moving cage, reaching

for tassels. I've picked cherries, scooped
pickles, sold knives and rakes and

rolls that fell to the floor, all
while my bosses took up flying.

Maybe Pagliacci's wouldn't be bad:
Evenings, a car, the minor streets

of Queen Anne. And at the end
of my shift, I could settle in—eating

what got sent back.

THE TABLE OF LOSSES

Both hands, both feet, both eyes,
a life. For these I'd receive

the Principal Sum, though there'd
be limitations, forms to fill out.

If it wasn't ptomaines, bacterial infection,
a self-inflicted wound or a war (declared

or not), I'd be referred to the Table
of Benefits, Class III, page 2. $20,000.00

isn't much, certainly not for the tears
(if eyes were not among the members

lost), barely enough to cover your bones,
my breasts. Already I've dug a hole

and begun to fill it: shared *couchette*
on the train to Rome (asked *sposato?*

we beamed like newlyweds), hike
to Yokum Ridge (when the trail

gave way to ice and rock, you climbed,
I watched). I'm in Bishop's boat—the one

with all the rainbows—fireweed, sky-
rocket, Indian paintbrush. Red shorts.

Blue bandana. Perfect arc of your back.

THE MOON

Though its map is drenched with watery names—
Lake of Dreams, Sea of Clouds, Bay of Dew—
the moon is waterless. Temperatures range
from three-hundred above to three-hundred below.
Rising 15,000 feet, the Apennines
stood up long before Galileo.

To sleep in the light of the moon is to weaken
your sight. The moon, the bushmen say,
is a man who angered the sun. Red because
Earth is in the way, "bloody" moons
portend catastrophe. To wax and wane
in Tierra del Fuego, the moon puts on and loses weight.

Evil, fickle, noble, ruler of Monday,
giver of dreams and home of broken vows,
mirror, silver candle, assembler of stars:
only astronauts have seen your dark, mysterious
side. Though in pictures it looks like more,
Aldrin's footprint didn't sink an inch.

Once, in Kansas, on a golf course white
with snow, I saw you through a telescope.
Your brightness sent Orion to bed. When a rock
arrived at the Trenton Museum, I skipped school
to stand in line. In the Wallowas and the Bitterroots,
through the lace of urban curtains, I've watched you rise.

O place of lunacy, wasted treasures, squandered
time. Confuser of noodles, poppy, sad guitar.
Think of oceans, think of the taste of tears.
What something far away can guide.

JENNIFER'S PEACHES CARDINAL HUME FOR THE PRIESTS AT WESTMINSTER CATHEDRAL

Half the time a miracle
not blowing up the kitchen,
not having the seeds
of mustard or poppy spurt
from an oily pan
like so many curses unbidden
(why doesn't the recipe mention lids?);
the rest of the time *excuse me for cooking!*
but the seeds keep right on popping,
or the oven explodes in a Mephistophelean
flash, smack dab in the middle
of fixing forty-garlic chicken—
sixteen peeled, twenty-four to go.
O, my St. Margaret puff pastry
poofed. O, my Toad-in-the-Hole kaput.
Something's missing. And he, not
stopping to swallow before he speaks:
Flavor? Do you think it might be flavor?

HOLLY HOCK BAKERY'S MOVING TO MADISON VALLEY

So she's leaving us, dear Holly, for blacker forests,
for banana cream more creamy, for exponentially irresistible tarts.

So long, loganberry seven layer. Bon voyage, apricot chiffon.
Going, going, cinnamon buckle, gone.

Suddenly the birds at her feeder look good enough to eat.
She corners a white-throated sparrow, crunches his pretzel stick bones.

Like a child stuffing saltines into her mouth, whistling a tune, she
Sam Peabody Peabody Peabodys—grief escaping like feathery crumbs.

THE SAUSAGE PARADE

When the Roman Empire, like an overcooked
kielbasa, began to shrivel up, Christians made them

illegal. Peperone, Calabrese, Sanguinaccio:
from speakeasy kitchens, butter, lard, and onion

hissed. Holsteiner, Genoa, Cervelats:
Twenty centuries later, the High-Production

Pickle Injector ensures a steady supply.
Presskopf, Figatelli, Jagdwurst:

could it be their names? That each must form
to its casing? Whose nose hasn't longed

for the scent of fennel and pork?
Who can say *sausage* isn't onomatopoeic?

"Cook them slowly," *Dishes of the World*
insists. "To keep from bursting, prick."

Robert was my first: red pepper, pimento
Pinch. Chorizo de Lomo. Taught me

sizzle, avoidance of smokehouse shrink. Never
would I settle for less. Byron Speer—oatmeal, vinegar

thyme—loved to go shirtless March to November.
Skin silken gravy, oven-baked. Chuck, a Drisheen—

running ox, tansy-tinged; two parts blood
to one part cream. Helmut, all-hands-in-the-pot

simmering shallots, 6' 2", 220, sweetness
soaked (lawyer by day, Braunschweiger

by night); Dylan a Rotwurst, *keeping sausage*—
sage, chestnut purée, lemon, Muscadet—

would have kept and kept ...

The man I love doesn't love my bread-crumb-soaked,
sputtering-pork-and-chipolata past—

salsicce, budini, zamponi.
But the past is long as Italy's boot.
It is made of leeks, red wine,
crushed garlic, whole peppercorns.

There is plenty of room at the table.

MY HOUR WITH JORIE GRAHAM

1.
I was supposed to buy her lunch.
All she wanted: the juice
of apples.

2.
Too-ripe fruit
slit with a Henckels.
Moths surrounding
the runoff.

3.
Her mouth at a bottle shaped like an apple
(my mouth mute as an apple)

4.
My poem my pomegranate my brand new outfit
(The poem asking *whose poem is it?*
The poem unsure)

5.
Hadn't I read Keats
Hadn't I heard of the objective correlative

6.
Let the siskins and the artichokes speak for themselves!

98,000.2.

God I hate this
(God in my mind of no mind God in the (swollen) sea & me without oars)

♉.
Just-butterfly—the wet & vulnerable hour
Butterfly shirking the worm's pedestrian hunger . . .

🕒.
all those layers
so many folds of gauzy black
I never did find where the fabric ended
(the fabric the thing concealing, the feeling untoward)
Draped like the partial torso of Iris
((((((of being wrong altogether, of her being altogether right))))))

💣💣💣.
What it must've been for Helen . . .
(war of the seeking not to estrange, war of the coveted
apple)

📂.
We paused on the sidewalk
talked course loads, needy students, summers in Wyoming
I asked did she still find time to write
(in this ivy rancor in these halls washed free of sepulchral leisure)

(☺).

She smiled the smile of transcendence

13.
Goddess of tossed back hair & dirt-smudged pumps
Pulse's impulse
Some first-year's wettest dream
Damned if I'd consciously take your advice
Damn if I still don't find the finest powder
where I brushed against your wings.

WHAT THE GRAD STUDENTS SAID

This is a terrific title, all your titles
should be this good—like a playground

with twirly and tunnel slides,
and a bathroom nearby to boot!

And all your poems should be as good
as this first one, which not only stood out

like a tilt-a-whirl on a flatbed broken down
along I-5, but reminded us of the words

we hate, like any compound adjective
and *scrunch*. We liked very much the one

with the Brain Gelatin Mold. Also, the one
where Bly loses his luggage along with his smiling-

Buddha shtick at the Dodge. However, we didn't
get interested until *gingivitis* and, overall, we stopped

reading when we realized—by the third line—
you weren't even trying to reach us at all but instead

yammering on to a nephew, son, sister, blah, blah, blah.
In other words, you weren't a finalist, runner-up, semi-finalist,

22nd or even 55th in line, but you were definitely
one of the 67 entrants! That, a little ketchup,

marmalade, vinegar, a few shakes of salt,
and a pinch of dried mustard will sure make a good

marinade for baby backs, but you thoroughly, definitely,
unredeemingly, did not in any way, shape,

or razzle-dazzle popsicle, come within
dozens of Mr. Natural paces from winning

our coveted prize.

JUST DON'T WRITE ANY POEMS ABOUT NIAGARA FALLS

~ *Richard Hugo*

Nobody cares it's raining where you are.
Nobody wants to know a cumulonimbus
floats by your house like a sneezing frog. Keep it

to yourself. Keep too your mother's mother's
labored-over pansies—ivory petals bowing
like sheets on a pulley clothesline, morning

glories strangling your will as guilelessly
as the sky. We've already read the one about
the hamster in the foxglove, so we won't

be alarmed when it turns out to be
a baby possum, nor will we stick around
for your *splendid marsupial triumphant evolution*

song. Nobody cares, in other words,
about your childhood: gargantuan zucchinis,
ailing mimosas, the day your father sliced

your beach ball with his pocket knife when it crushed
a struggling tomato; Snooper and Peeka, Ashes and Butch;
your various hunches as to the origins of a large, rectangular-

with-round-depression rock, perfect birdbath for grackles
and starlings: Lenape bed pan, meteor, Yapese dime.
If we have to read one more time about your return

to Grove Ave. in the spring of '95, finding your bubble-gum pink
and ever-lintful hyacinth choking beneath the vent for the dryer,
or imagine your breaking voice as you grope to describe

the stranger among your Uncle Peter's wrapped-in-the-*Kansas-City
Star*-and-carried-from-Tightwad-Missouri comfrey (comfrey
which proceeded to blanket the entire yard), if you then not

so surreptitiously segue into tales of two-foot snows
cushioning your *N*'s (*Needs Improvement,* you got them in
"Follows Directions"); stroke, in other words, that tiniest violin

of a weatherful, kittenful, puppyful, *o great vanished youth,*
grandmother-inspired yarn, and we're cursing you:
in your next life you'll be the maintenance guy

at Niagara Falls in ticking coveralls, name embroidered
above your heart—the one in charge of the Giant Valve,
releasing pressure for newlyweds and tourists, ensuring

water flows at a rate they can gush at. When they've finished
(*what a beautiful day, the day we met . . . I'm so glad your grandma
let slip her passion for miniature poodles . . . Snuggles would love

this place! Did I ever tell you I came here as a child . . .*), when
they want to know if it's worth springing for a valentine tub
or a boat ride to the Cave of the Winds and the trilobite wall,

you'll be the one they turn to for advice.

WHAT I MEANT TO SAY BEFORE I SAID "SO LONG"

~ for Dante Alfredo Silano

There will be spiders the size of your ears, drinks
that will make you stupid, matches you'll long
to strike; there will be mop-ups the size of Rhode Island.

Or you'll be driving at night beneath the cloud-hidden
Perseids, but the car in front will lose a wheel, spray
a million sparks. The spider won't drop its strand

above your bed but choose a far corner. Don't kill it:
what it spins will rival what hangs from your neighbor's
hedge. Your father loves what shines—the flash

in the pan, two-penny nugget glint, what might lead him
from buckets, latex, brush's swish, loves the gleam
that was you in his eye. As a child he built fires

beneath a rising Dog Star, ignored the heat,
his mother's no's, heard only *go ahead, Matty-boy,*
my tee-too, my shaver, build whatever you like.

Loved what was left when the brightness died,
to fish the yard for the stubs of rockets. What he kindled
in Ash Flat—eight miles from Evening Shade, lift of Earth

that is Ozarks—he feeds logs to now (last stop being the flashing
CHAINS REQUIRED), where the spark between him
and your mother . . . where you were born. Ashland.

Which must be why they named you Dante, an unlit match
held close to a blaze. He pans for gold, tells us by the crow's
fly (by the eagle, by the osprey) we're close to a mine, scars

in the side of a hill, close to where the flood of '64 tore the earth,
unearthed the glimmers he dreams of. He's got scars on his back,
stretches of road he can't recall but don't be scared: all that fire-

water's behind him, the bottomless tap, beer after golden beer.
His love for explosives cost him all the gold in the Applegate Valley,
"Possession of a firearm" emblazoned on screens from Metuchen

to Tucson—*a pellet gun; I shot at the sky*. Not that we're here
forever, not that we don't live in the shadow of live volcanoes,
the chance we'll wake to at least a dusting of ash. *So long,*

trooper, I managed to say, your father asking for Roman Candles,
Dancing Bees, Flower Clusters, *stuff that shoots out sparks.*
South of Eugene, two hundred miles from your eager hands,

the sun through clouds a million motionless searchlights,
I began to fall in a trap: *Don't let boredom grip you*
the way you gripped my finger; let even the seemingly

starkest places yield you Black-Eyed Susans; learn from the woman
who with her entire body tells you "I've done all this."
Since each of us will soon be part of the meal,

since we're more like tents than mountains, and mountains
disappear . . . (spinning, sinking, fuel light an ember,
finally sputtering out).

AT THE SHOREBIRD FESTIVAL: GRAYS HARBOR COUNTY, WASHINGTON

We're learning their names: dunlin, black-bellied plover.
Sandpipers: western and least. Styles of probing:
run, stop, run; incessant sewing machine. What's
diagnostic: upturned bill of the slender, elegant
avocet. Ruddy turnstone's crimson feet.

Wired for wind and cold, bills conveniently tuck
beneath scapulars; feet retreat to feathered bellies.
At the slightest hint of shadow, sudden movement
(ring-billed gull, drifting leaf), they take to the air
like giant swirling amoebas, locust dark till they turn

in a flash of white—beautiful, undulant whirl
lowering the odds of a raptor's successful strike;
mournful *tu tu tu* of dowitcher, raucous *cur-ret* of the knot
translating unmistakably: *watch out*. Every movement,
ounce, sound, rigged for survival. But we're not thinking

life or death, the why of insulation, skittishness. We're focused,
as always, on something else: *American coot, osprey near bridge
to Aberdeen* (mill stench, strip mall, though equaling loss, unworthy
of note), a nearby curmudgeon's grumble ("the brochure said
thousands . . ."), what's for lunch—mortality's access,

like the nesting grounds of snowy plovers,
all but permanently blocked. Even when we turn
from mudflat to ocean, to the surfer stuck in a crisscross
of breakers refusing to spit him out—bobbing, waving his arms—
to four Jeep Cherokees emblazoned "Ocean Shores Police"

barreling down the beach, to a man—wild-eyed, mustachioed—
heading out in a boat to save him, routine, we're thinking.
And as he guns the motor, greets each surge—head high,
bulging chest—as he enters the whirling churn,
we're unconcerned enough to admire

the sunlight pouring down in silvery rays,
magnificent concert of every-which-way waves.
Even when two massive swells converge to flip his boat,
and *he's* the one who's waving *I'm okay.* Rising. Falling.
Disappearing. Surf a vortex . . . rushes . . . rips . . .

Just as we're getting nervous (police, walkie-talkies, a growing,
gawking crowd), *was he wearing a wetsuit isn't ten minutes all it takes?*
out of nowhere a Coast Guard lifeboat nabs the surfer,
while a faint, growing louder, whir-and-heart-pounding-
clomp-clomp-clomp of a chopper lowers in

on the place where . . . *but now I don't see him is he
he's under* blinding swirl of water and blades,
a man on a rope plunging into *he can't be did you see
his eyes did you see* the squall, comes up with a body,
a body, limp as a . . . limp as a . . .

he's okay, the wind knocked out that's all hoists him up
like a half-mast flag on a windless day *he sure looks
dead like a dead man have you ever seen someone living
hang like that like the suit's empty* to shore where medics
he'll be okay those who knew him cradling their own

incredulous faces, a round of *shits* pacing static *no response* no one asking *is he?* Huddled. Stunned. Light draining the sky. The last *good God. Goodnight.* Even after the tide erases every footprint, and where he lay a flock of whimbrels alights.

SUCH A WAY TO GO

But that's how it is. One minute battling traffic. Next, head
in an oven, inner kingdom hospital blue—cool and soothing

glacier, what a baby boy comes home in. With a sparkling
silver toothbrush, the blanket's unsinged. De-ashed. Daisy

Marble, Butter Sponge removed. And what satisfaction!
Such blue brilliance—spent comets, star cinders—loosened

with Ajax. With force. No wonder she chose this: rising
crescents, soft braids, perfect white. Left her children

(bread and milk). The pan too large. Under. Over. Not
quite done. Tick and bang of a cold place heating.

Head where flour, water, salt. Peaks before they fell.

THEY'RE PROHIBITED BY CITY ORDINANCE

but if I were a horse, I'd eat like one.
Face against the wind, win you over

with my longing for apples. I'd be skittish,
with my own particular fears. Saddle-

flinching. Cantering, but only when you want me
to trot. If I were a horse, I'd be proud

of all sixteen of my hands. Which hay,
which paths, when to be put out to pasture:

I'd know. You'd be braiding red yarn into my tail,
warning others I kick, blaming my meanness

on the apples. And I'd kick you. I'd kick you.

IN THAT OTHER UNIVERSE

I married you—all your useless
gadgets, all your mother's wishes
I were Jewish, all my almost perfect
birthday poundcakes, all your kindness,
all your kindness (all my doubts).

Our best man brought the abalone
rings, snow peas, *rughetta*, chanterelles.
My best friend caught the broccoli flowerets.

After the stroll through spaghetti,
hubbard, and delicata, after the artichoke
toss and pin the turnip on the navel,
after the toasts and the long good-bye,
we honeymooned on an island
ninety miles along where long-

necked stilts predicted falsely our demise.
Days we'd shop for chervil, capsicum, basil.
Nights we'd point to constellations—cilantro,
asparagus, savory. We thought of having everyone

for dinner, then listened to the tui. We thought
of having everyone: the sleeping sea gull, head
tucked under a wing, the bones of emus.

We thought of sending invitations: come as you are,
tomato. And rock wren, riflebird, gannet: RSVP.
And the waves began to whisper *Good choice,
Good choice, Good choice,* in that other universe,
on a planet like a patty-pan squash.

TO THE WOMAN WHO, WHEN I WENT TO HEAT MY PIZZA IN THE OFFICE MICROWAVE, ASKED ME, "WHO ARE YOU?"

I am ranked the Highest Order, Most Benevolent
Devilled Eggs, i.e., Most Honored Toothless Machu Picchu,
gracious Queen of Ouzel Dust. I was voted Most Likely
to Hug a Flammable Ranch and Miss Grow a Sputnik
on Your Face. In church I drink the spots
from Lucy Spigman's dress. In Bartell Drugs I pray
to muscle rub. Before you now I place an artist's sketch,
fully rendered, fully built of horsehair lamps
and an orange couch (40% broasted, 40% rapeseed,

30% duff). I invented the perpetually grieving
Linzer torte and the self-effervescing cat-box lid.
I am first in Oil of Amphibian samovars, Silly Putty
tabletops, and sipping sprigs. I've yet to lose
a carob-coated raisin race, and I finished 45th at 23rd
and 61st at 3.2.8. I know, in short, of ants who'll eat
an earwig's leg for lunch. Regrettably, I've never
owned a boat, but I've seen Helen Farkus flinch.
Rest assured: documents I carry prove my worthiness.

MEN OF THE STONE AGE HAD NO USE FOR FRACTIONS

Neither do I. Who wants a piece
of cracker, chocolate cookie bite?
Who wants what's left at the bottom of the bag?
Give me the whole hog.
Give me salt pork, fat back, jowls.
Give me knuckles and cracklings, headcheese and lard.
Let me lick the grease from my fingers,
then lie on a couch, sated, lambent-lipped, no room to squeeze
a quarter ounce.

Spare me the snippets, shavings, scraps.
Spare me nips and drams.
Not the clause but the sentence.
Not the sentence but the tome.
(No piece without its pieces; no part without its whole.)

Give me the fish with the head intact.
Let me stare at the eye—never-melting hailstone, tapioca pearl.
Give me the eggs and their shells—blood spot, albumen.
Give me the skillet carried by covered wagon, Maverick, U-Haul.
Baltimore non-stick. Whippany Teflon.

Whatever a shebang is, I want it.
And leave in the pits, the seeds, the core.
Bring me everything and don't peel it.
(The crumbs I'll feed to the crows).

TOO SMALL FOR INTELLECT, BIG ENOUGH FOR LOVE

~ *early 20th-century obstetrics text describing a woman's brain*

My grandmother wasn't a chemist, but in her kitchen I learned
precision, science of dollop, pinch. She didn't own

a thermometer, measured heat with a dab to her wrist.
Yeast foamed like the incoming tide at Love Ladies Beach,

like drops of HCl in a test-tube filled with zinc. Kneaded
not by machine so that now I can't enter my kitchen, touch

bowl, sugar, flour, wooden spoon without her long-earned
confidence dissolving the shame of a hundred chem lab flops:

scales so sure weight changed with a breeze, easily smashed
pipettes, terror of Bunsen burner, meniscus more a reason

to pause (water smiling!). Without her hands on mine:
feel how that feels? Now you're ready for rising.

TOWARD AN UNDERSTANDING OF MY SO-CALLED CALLING

It's my mother's fault.
When I squirmed in church,
craned to count, on the bridges

of stern parishioners, horn rims
and cat eyes; when I looked up,
not in search of light or truth,

but to fill the wooden beams
with loopy, imagined script;
when her glance, which I'm sure

could stop me now, failed to halt
my swinging legs, she'd grab her purse
(an eye on me, an eye on the priest),

dig past needles, rows of knit and purl,
lipstick bright as flamingos, ubiquitous
tissues, the silvery rain hat folded down

to one thick, snapped-down strip, hand me
paper and pen. Blame my father, post-cookout
star-gazer, astronomically enthusiastic (*lots*

of kids have burgers; how many Seven Sisters?),
who taught the comfort of wandering
Cassiopeia. The ones that moved, he said,

were ours. Blame them both, their painstaking
passions—infinitesimal, all-consuming,
pointless as too-far-off-to-warm-us stars,

as a great-great-grandmother's tightly woven
bun, which though I never saw it unfurl,
was rumored to fall to her knees.

THE 1238 CHERRY AVENUE CREDO

I believe in waking early—effortless drift from dream to dawn
like a browned-in-the-oven loaf. First light on a pink brick wall.
There's nothing wrong with hand-me-downs, fog, getting lost
in a flame. I'm not convinced, in the event of a water landing,
seat cushions will save us, or that childhood hamsters ever die.
I vote no for ostrich rides, bowling where the scoring's computerized.
You gotta earn your bread and butter, my Polish grandmother says.
Make mine crusty Italian, rosemary-riddled, extra-virgin dipped.

SPELLCHECK CHANGES *SILANO* TO *SALINE*

but I don't mind—ever-tearful,
ever-nicknamed Pickles Queen.
Lover of brine—splash zone,
pelagic, sub-littoral. Home
where the ocean's near. Ever
drawn to the true point
of beginning—horseshoe crabs
on a Wildwood beach, crinoid lilies
swaying shallowly. What, after all,
is *Silano*? Father's father's father's. . .
eighteen *greats* to Senator Eppio,
richest of Roman blood, but just
one quarter, while under a tugging sea—
Katrosh, Bullock, Pickarski. *Mother's
maiden name, please* (underside
of who we are, shadow self, whispering).
With a name like Saline maybe I'd befriend
the crepuscular thick knees, glimpse
magellanic plover's bright Chilean feet.
Rise each dawn to the probing marks
of sanderlings while floating up
from the surf the almost-audible tunes
of murmuring sirens—*bulka, kapusta, shushpie*.
Might ease the final trip to Graveyard Spit,
ashes scattered near sticky daisy, sand verbena,
rocket pea, bill of the pirouetting phalarope.

FROM

BLUE POSITIVE

(2006)

BLUE POSITIVE

To begin I need to tell you about Phoenix, who's telling me he's so hungry
he could eat twenty sumo wrestlers, diapers and all. I need to tell you
about these puke-yellow walls, about Ms. Potthoff, how she shines

in this cluttered, chalk-choked room like the Iowa sun in July, cares for these kids
like they care about their class pet Lizzy, a spotted gecko; I need you to see
Christabel's two-inch navy-blue fingernails, who wrote *for even your father*

was once a stranger; also smiling Myra, who tells us Celtic music's
like holding a cat, like taking her first bath, like her brother
and sister being born. I need to take off

this scratchy sweater, put on my old gray sweatshirt, fraying at the seams,
the zipper about to go. I need to tell you about the white boot
that used to be my sister's, then mine, then my little brother's

as he hopped home, one foot bare, one still-warm boot stuck
in the neighbor's drifting snow. Arnold says
it's like the colors of a Mexican sky,

a tarpon's glistening fin, while Jamar, Jamar says we should all have, like the dog
whose owner always gives him the last piece of poppy-seed cake,
a quiet place to lie down. Listening,

I hear the waves off the coast of St. Ives, where gannets, common as pasties, stretched
every inch of their seventy-two-inch spans. Listening, I need to take you
to the Seep Lakes late, very late on the night of the Leonids,

my son with a cold, so in all the photos, where my best friend Lisa Sylvester
said an angel had shushed me, had shushed us all, a glistening,
which is why I must tell you of Dr. Lydia Adler's

gloved and sterile hands, how I slid out blue, but blue positive; my mother's blood
the rain; if we could see it but we can't, the sky, Ayla says, isn't crying;
the sky never cries. Our burdens are small,

or just the right size. I wore a red and black corduroy jumper, in a lavender dress,
sipped wine—a little of hers, a little of theirs, like those seeping lakes,
seeping into mine.

THIS IS NOT THE LAST POEM ABOUT PEARS

and certainly not the first,
but I'm not talking
about D'Anjous, Comices,
Boscs, the ones you find
at a Safeway or a Food Lion
while under Muzak's spell,
pears which are sometimes sweet
like a kiss on the lips after many kisses
on the cheek, but more often not—
are like gnawing on the branch of a willow.
No. I'm talking about a pear from a tree
in your own yard, where rain, sun, and wind,
the occasional, inadvertent stumble
of a spider or an ant are all that has touched it.
And, at the very beginning, the petals,
on a rainy, or sunny, or windy day
which fall all at once like laundry
fresh from the spinning wash.
When they fall they leave behind
hundreds of parasols not unlike
the ones you saw as you gazed into pond water
under a microscope. Over the summer,
whether you notice or not,
they swell to miniature blowfish
but your father says, each time you ask,
not yet, so while rodents, bees, birds, worms . . .
you wait till he pulls in the drive and,
instead of heading straight for a nap,
joins you, picks one up—his tired body holding
the scent of machinery overworked—

looks it over, points to the one place not
worm-riddled, squirrel-gnawed,
hornet-bored, grackle-pecked:
Here, try that. It could've been mealy.
You could have swallowed
thorax, stinger, rotting flesh.
Instead your mouth is honored,
in a single bite, by a tiny planet
sweetened by a father's
immeasurable sacrifice.

MOTHER OF PEACE

but no quiet—
Puccini, Patsy Cline,
Some Enchanted Evening,
effervescing from unstoppable lips,
the unpieced quilt—
Texas Troubles—
tabled twenty years
as she presses her foot
to the Singer's pedal, inching along
the rickrack of a hooded dress
while I doze on the bed,
intermittent surges stirring.
Mother of wisdom—
vinegar/lemon in lieu of Windex,
jelly most un-petroleum.
Matriarch of markets—
resurrecting last week's beets,
overseer of kugel, *kapusta*, kale.
Queen of the tooth-chipping
biscotti, triple baked.

Mother of pizzicato
and pasta, the war
against throw away.
Resilient reassurer,
religiously renegade,
refuser of old age.

Little red hen gone global.
Teeny tiny woman with her teeny tiny bone
shirking her osteo-hunch. Woman who lived
in the pastel-pink, snakeskin pump.

Mother of *right to the moon* and *don't you dare,
I'll give ya's* and *so's your Aunt Lizzies,*
serving, on Easter, all Arkansas,
then cracking hickories for the Christmas loaf,
clues to the Sunday puzzle, digging around

for the root of nasturtium, the why
of Silano. Mother of peace
but no quiet. Dress
I wriggled into,
never took off.

MY WORDS

I never liked *pachyderm*, especially when I learned elephants are anything
but thick-skinned. Ditto to the dowdily galumphing *dromedary*
with its root in *dromad*, Greek for swift.

Ones I never considered memorable or strange—
bubble, banana, anemone—bloomed
when my son began to use them

to describe falling snow, a crescent moon,
a cockatiel's plume. *Plum* is a terrible
word for a perfect fruit, *summer*

beautiful as the cold and empty beach we stroll nine months
of the year. I like *gingivitis* and *gaggle*. *Gizzard,* too—
it must be all that ga ga goo—must be,

if not primal, crib-al, must harken back to days
pre-list, pre-who-is-this-this-
in-the-mirror? Pre-must-do.

I wanted *gourds* and *ghouls*; I wanted *gargantuan galas*,
gherkins galore, but really what I wanted
was that somersaultingly salty

source, to return to a time when my skin
was transparent, when water
was my word.

MY MAN WITH HIS FLY REEL EYES

~ *After Andre Breton*

My man with his fly reel eyes
Pale morning dun desire

My man's hip-wader heat
Gravel-in-the-shallows drive

My man with his Yakima Canyon shoulders
Sagebrush brow

My man's fingerling tongue
Biceps smooth as skipping stones

My man with his sockeye sperm
Trunk of ponderosa

My man's teeth the snow-fresh tracks
of cougar—cougar scream & cougar silence

My man's Frenchmen Coulee hands
My man the hawk with a snake in its mouth

My man the trout growing larger
My man skunked—his cattail want

My man the 40-mile-an-hour gust
a tarp set free from rocks

TRAVELER'S LAMENT

Should we have stayed at home and dreamed of here? Where should we be today?
       ~ Elizabeth Bishop

I miss the man who sells us wine, suggests
the Covey Run,

Rainbow Grocery's neon orange tennis ball
tangerine stacks.

I miss the flower shop with its bundles of African Daisies,
Queen Anne's Lace.

I miss our street, gossamer blossoms stuck like unlucky insects
to windshields, headlights.

I even miss the neighbor's pick-up turning over, at six am,
like twenty Hoovers and a leaf blower,

clang of dumpster lid. Futility of sweeping sunflower hulls
from the walk,

the mailman bringing (politely, almost daily) more and more
of nothing.

I miss lugging the trash to the curb in a robe
about to slip open.

The hot water tank we easily emptied
each time we made love in the tub.

SALVAGING JUST MIGHT LEAD TO SALVATION

so when you come home there's a tickle in my throat what should I take
is there tea? Could you make it with honey? Could you bring me an aspirin a pillow all
the *New Yorkers*? Could you turn up the heat so we almost choke?
& the remote? Could you stick a Coke in the freezer? I do

& when I come home with a headache the size of New Hampshire you go oh my sweet
sweet square root of three my tikka masala poppadum chutney-dipped
let me get you a patch of blue a stratocumulus don't move

so when you come home at noon in a suit going yeah I know I know I got fired
I'm all ears those bastards! they don't know who they're losing
but didn't you say you weren't anywhere close to a window
& how about those cubicles

so when I come home with a nasty note from a student *you're not fostering
my learning* you tell me there's a present for me on the couch & when I get there
it's a what-really-counts-is-letting-them-stand-in-another-person's-
tossed-from-a-speeding-car-and-sitting-on-the-freeway's shoes

which also means after months of *we'll let you know*s and *we'll call you*s on the day
I say honey maybe you should call the folks at Parker Personnel you get the job
& it's the right one the one you've always wanted & when you pop
the cork unbelievably I catch it all the dogs convening
a crazy canine chorus praising perseverance luck

which means when some god of the classroom lets me slip into improv zone
& I'm on a roll & there's this buzz and they're getting it! they're getting
what it means to have all been to Auburn but not one of them to Fife
that they all hated their 2nd grade teachers but love baked beans
Lyle Lovett windy nights you know to bring me not only

#2 pencil yellow African daises exam-book blue
forget-me-nots and fresh as a brand new roster
lilies but to tell all the guys at the poker table
I'm the best teacher in all King County

which means when my card slides out from the little slot WE CANNOT PROCESS
YOUR ACCOUNT TRY AGAIN LATER you're ready with your card & when
the money you made tagging fish in the Bering Sea dries up and disappears
I pay for the yellow finns jalapeños tortillas turtle beans & God forbid

we need to go back on food-stamps I'll stand in line at DSHS
Cabrini? I can almost taste it while you head off to Our Lady
of the Dunes melt the Velveeta till it's almost brie

which means we've stopped keeping track of who paid for what who bought table
skillet spoon who'll fork it up for the rent who scratched broke dirtied
tangled what focus instead on averting fights fending them off
like nasty germs that are hell on a throat on a life

& when really we want to say *you're selfish you're so fucking selfish* I'm selfish but
if you'd wipe the counters put out the trash or on the one nice thing
they did that day week month or even yes a fight a good one
real juicy not lugging up 88-year-old phlegm but new stuff
like don't tell me when I'm bloated or starting every
other raging sentence *you*

& now and then so horrible it ends in tears me of course wailing almost screaming
you're the wrong person I made a mistake I hate you I hate you
but because you're there to hold me a miracle my pea brain
maybe he really really does love me won't leave which doesn't

mean he won't which doesn't mean this way
of taking care is for everyone or only for hets
or like I'm advocating some kind of morality
Anita Bryant fresh-squeezed homophobic
takeover or even that single people
are inherently unhappy mistaken
or downright lost

but that maybe we're meant like great-crested grebes mouths dripping slimy weeds
lifting erect or the bird of paradise that clears on the forest floor a place to lift glinting
wings to waltz twirl leap to land on a mate he'll keep though yes it's oversimplifying
anthropomorphizing is not the way
a red-winged blackbird colony operates

but if we're to trust the eyes and ears of anthropologists & scientists over 90%
of birds & humans are monogamous though I'm not 100% sure they're including
the Choctaw, Crow, Cherokee, Creek, Pawnee, Minitari, & Arichara
for whom the husband weds not just his wife

but aunts & nieces too kinship increasingly matted a woven mesh precariously dan-
gling not too unlike a bushtit nest till *this situation ends in IX*
(MB = B; MBW = BW) for any "a" is MB though
I bet it makes sense if it's all you know
like asking Emily Post
or the tribal elders

though it probably isn't true for every stomped on wine glass borrowed or blue
for every groped for garter tossed bouquet sweetheart neckline Bertha collar
or leg-of-mutton sleeve there's a Moulay Ismail emperor of Morocco
siring 888 children from upwards of 200 wives or the Tiwi nubile

whose privates are poked with a spear her future son-in-law
strokes hugs calls *wife* in this way marrying
all her unborn daughters

which means there's a chance you too might want someone who'll buy more Kleenex
tell you your tea is steeped shirt's wrinkled tag's hanging out
who swipes with licked finger the ketchup from your cheek
who tells you my you're looking pale knows how to raise
your drooping head

though I know you might be asking *marriage?! are you fucking kidding? I just want some pussy!* which I don't blame you for at all especially since there's a strong argument
we're more like the forgivably polygamous lion than a bunch of birds
a case to be made for a male to spread his seed
which is not to say every woman
craves monogamy

no matter how much our behavior resembles hornbills hoopoes meercats cobras
or moral owls I'm not about to tell you marriage is easy or difficult
or a hocus pocus fantasy only breeders want or know
not about to tell you it's for you

girls traded for coconuts chariots shields yams all of it resting on capture
hope-chests painstaking lace I'd almost say resist it in homage to all
those wasted lives all those hours filling trousseaux
before a father could breathe a relief-ful sigh
I'd almost say stay single don't get stuck
like my grandmother says
washing some guy's
shorts

except I've always been drawn to the scraggliest plant on the shelf
leggy zucchini contorted delphinium mangiest chard
to fixing what just might have a second life
can't stand not trying to resurrect
a broken fan into could I?
a hotdog grill?

to taking a heap of a '61 Caddy spray-painted gold
half-reclaimed by Ozark mud
digging the damn thing out.

DEFINE MEDICAL TERMINOLOGY AND CONDITIONS ASSOCIATED WITH CONCEPTION

let's just say right now it's a wonder
sperm & egg found a way to fuse at all
that godforsakenly cold and drizzly day
gravelly jerky mud-puddled rutted all-too-jolting ride
icy bike seat jutting my miracled mound
for anything close to fertilization
lull and bob of a zygote (23 his, 23 mine)
though I must admit I never understood
Miss Barbieri's *oogenesis*
which sounded more
like someone about to come
than *formation of a haploid ovum*

Normally Tiger Mountain's the rising trills of orange-crowned warblers
yellow-rump's quick-witted whirs
Pacific Slope's *eeeeoooit!*
but today except for occasional winter wren bursts
it's silent

Fitting perhaps
silence lichen-drenched
allowing a chance to take it all in
this bumpy gelid finger-numbing ride
this steep slog up loose rock
every-which-way rain
ruts slicks big sticks old snow
where it looks and feels
like maybe March
no sign at all of gooseberry's

fuschia-starred tips
not even the leaves of *Trillium* . . .
Had to stop
near the top
push to a flattish spot
Hop on
Continue up

My guess?
In that pause
half in the clouds
half not
green shoots not yet dangling
bleeding hearts
in the late-spring mist
one persistent sperm
a hundred million confreres weakening
the egg's insistent lock
pushed like a coho
sniffing home
from a thousand miles

From here it hardly seems conceivable
not only the hostile environment
elevation makes
but the one I've made
twenty years internally
diaphragm & spermicide
dependable dauntless intruders
on any sperm or egg's design

Today's a first in fact
so I'm extra carefully tasting
when we reach the top
my husband's salty cheeks tongue lips
50 degrees warmer
than my hands
which hold his head
not forgetting to mention
we've beaten (again)
the odds . . .

CROWN OF SONNETS FOR A SON

1.
For this I've waited very long.
Waited, knowing little. And little did I know,
when first you settled in, I'd bleed. Didn't know
I'd crave pad thai, fish tacos, that strong-
willed, flat-tummied me as distant as dawn
just after sunset flashes green. You'd grow,
they said, from grain, to pea, to bean before I'd show,
but three weeks in I traded buttons for drawstrings.
I crawled, breast-stroked; you lapped at newly teeming lakes.
Twin pink hyacinths bloomed beside the fence; you sprouted lungs.
Praising your poppy-seed heart, your father rearranged the spice rack,
imagined you five, seasoning stream-caught trout. Headaches
did their best that spring to keep me dumb
but slowly I bungled toward instinct, making sense of facts.

2.
Slowly I bungled toward instinct, making sense of facts,
cuz really I needed both: to not just
accept, for instance, my baking bun was the size of a dust
mite, had a rudimentary spine, but that not a scrap
of will, not one neuron's worth of thought,
nothing, in short, I'd done (except to follow lust)
sprang to life. Slowly. Toward trust.
And as they split and split, so too our half-life of loss.
Before the trip to the store for the test,
before I peed in a cup (o so very positive),
my cheeks were vodka-rosy, Merlot-tinged.
Now when I spot a cardinal's crimson crest
or any speck of red, I rub my belly (*please live . . .*);
now, like Procyon to its aging twin, we're hinged.

3.
Now, like Procyon to its aging twin, we're hinged—
my mid-day almond snack your sustenance,
though soon enough you'll blurt *It's chance—
parents shmarents . . . arbitrary!* (Singeing
as I've singed). And when you roll your eyes at my orange
scarf, and when you want a certain pair of jeans
I'll venture back to this: a single, chirping finch, first green,
pump-handle call of a jay; I'll binge,
in other words, on memory stripped of fear,
on how I'll guess I used to live.
Then I'll shell out eighty bucks for Levis
you'll throw in a backyard pool and sear
with chlorine—white-speckled galaxies.
(Why is it I can't wait to hear you cry?)

4.
Why is it I can't wait to hear you cry
or coo, to say (distinctly) *ghee?* Pushing,
contractions, dilation, hospital's rush rush:
who needs it? (Me.) Week four I named you Ry;
each time I told a friend, imagined cramps.
Hid my growing womb, but gushed
to those who knew (*This week the spleen goes in!*). O luscious
naps: each afternoon I happily succumbed.
But when Stewart and Belle—our city's parent peregrines—
took turns knocking pigeons from the sky,
keeping their wobbly eyases warm, I swore
I'd never be *that* animal—that one-
tracked. Or understand their bobbing, beaky fear.
As for a higher—human—intelligence, I'm less sure.

5.
As for a higher—human—intelligence, I'm less sure,
especially here with your father, twenty feet above me
in a tree—face scrunched, forehead holding
a nest box firmly as he screws it in.
Never mind the snow like darting pins.
Never mind the temperature (six or seven, at best).
The kestrels, come May, will need a place to nest.
And though there's no guarantee they'll choose this tree,
I toss a bag of shavings he spreads on the floor
to lure them in. Not that we ever know
what or who will successfully breed—slow
sperm, unfused tubes, collapsing wombs, peril
of aging eggs. Today you weigh six potato chips;
I try to laugh at what I can't control.

6.
I try to laugh at what I can't control—
take hormonal ups and downs. One week I wept incessantly
at diaper ads, Stevie Wonder's "Isn't She Lovely?",
Peter Falk's old raincoat, road-kill squirrels.
Then (for no apparent reason), crawled up
like a hibernating mole, sobbing uncontrollably
till I remembered lunch with a friend. I grabbed my keys
and off I went—as if all of this were normal.
Later when I told your dad he seemed concerned.
Don't worry, I quipped, he doesn't grow ears till next week.
In truth, I worry more than laugh. Can't
fathom the news I'm not carrying a genetic mistake,
a vegetable, a something with holes in his heart.
You can lower the odds, but nothing's 100 percent.

7.
You can lower the odds, but nothing's 100 percent,
not snipping a piece of tissue surrounding this little prawn,
not amnio's endless needle, swearing off caffeine,
aspirin, alcohol. Adjust to paying rent
on a home you'll never own, to a screened-in
porch so riddled with moths you can't see in.
To cleanse their hearts and minds, the Lakota enter
a womb of mud they fill with steaming stones.
As the heat becomes unbearable they pray
to their mothers, focus on the pain of giving birth,
on the drum keeping time to an ancient song.
Will I learn to live with a fear that never leaves?
This floating fetus its own mysterious Earth.
For this I've waited very long.

GETTING KICKED BY A FETUS

Like right before you reach your floor, just
before the door of an elevator opens.
Like the almost imperceptible
springs you waded through
in Iroquois Lake.
Carbonation.
Twitch.

Sometimes high and jabby near the ribs;
sometimes low and fizzy like a pie
releasing steam, like beans
on the stovetop—slow
simmer,

like the shimmer of incoming tide—hot, soft sand
meeting waves, slosh bringing sand crabs
that wriggle invisibly in.

And sometimes a school of herring
pushing through surf,
or a single herring

caught from a pier like a sliver of moon rising in the west;
sometimes a tadpole stuck in a pond growing smaller
and smaller, a puddle of mud, squirmy like worms—
now your left, now your right. Sometimes

neon flickering, like that Texaco sign near Riddle, Oregon—
from a distance it read TACO, but up close
the faintest glow, an occasional E or X,
like an ember re-igniting.

Like seeing your heartbeat through the thinnest part
of your foot, sunken well between ankle and heel,
reminder of a world beneath your skin, world
of which you know little,

and the pond growing smaller and smaller, soon the rolling waves
like the ones you dove into at Bradley Beach, at Barneget,
growing less frequent, your giant ocean
drying up, your little swimmer

sinking, giving way
to the waves
of his birth.

SONG FOR A NEWBORN

Oh my Double Thick Pork Chop,
my Prawn Tequila-kissed,
Most Pico of Pico de Gallos:
bless your brain—
its fluids & aqueducts, its ventricles,
the little fountains splashing.
Bless your arms which hang,
outstretched, in sleep,
as if conducting an orchestra,
a tune I'll never know.
Bless your capillaries
like the roots of Early Girls,
your large intestine like dozens
of miniature knackwursts.
Bless your liver, its 500 functions.
Bless your sternum, your scapula—
heck: bless all your 206 bones.
Someday you'll understand the humor
of an opening refrigerator eliciting
the Pope's voice, the irony of a logging saw
painted with grizzly bears, towering conifers,
a bright blue river, but for now I'll have to settle,
my Sugar-Cane Showered Scallop, my Swimming Angel,
for your smile which says Braised Chicken,
Cilantro Dumplings, Romaine's Most Tender Hearts.

HARBORVIEW

By the roots of my hair some god got hold of me
      ~ Sylvia Plath

By the roots of my hair, by the reinforced elastic
of my floral Bravado bra, by the fraying strands

of my blue-checked briefs, some god's gotten hold of me,
some god's squeezed hard the spit-up rag of my soul, rung me

like the little girl who rang our doorbell on Halloween, took
our M&Ms *is your baby okay? Why did they take him away?*

Some god's got me thinking my milk's poison, unfit
for a hungry child, some god's got me pacing,

set me flying like the black felt bats dangling
in the hall, some god so that now I can't trust my best friend's

healing hands, the Pad Thai she's spooning beside the rice (ditto
to the meds the doctors say will help me sleep) *Poison poison!*

as if the god who's got hold of me doesn't want me
well, doesn't want my rapid-fire brain to slow,

wants this ride for as long as it lasts, wants to take it
to its over-Niagara-in-a-barrel end, which is where

this god is taking me, one rung at a time, one ambulance,
one EMT strapping me in, throwing me off this earth,

cuz I've not only killed my son but a heap of others too.
Some god's got me by my shiny golden locks, by my milk-

leaking breasts, got me in this hospital, wisps like white scarves
circling my head, wisps the voices of men *back to bed you whore!*

Some god till I'm believing I've been shot, guts dribbling out,
till I'm sure I've ridden all over town in a spaceship, sure

I'm dead, a ghost, a smoldering corpse, though not before I'm holding up
a shaking wall, urging the others to help me (a plane about to land

on our heads), though soon enough thrown down by two night nurses,
strapped to a bed, though for weeks the flowers my in-laws sent

charred at the tips (having been to hell and back), clang of pots,
hissing shower, the two blue pills my roommate left in the sink,

all signals of doom, though some god got hold of me,
shook and shook me long and hard, she also brought me back.

EXPLAINING CURRENT EVENTS TO A ONE-YEAR-OLD

The sky will never be this gray—belly of a mallard,
body of a plane emerging from clouds—
layer upon layer in every direction.

Gone are the goldfinches, barn swallows, violet greens.
Welcome the juncos, their metronome calls,
welcome the play of light and dark,

the occasional patch of blue, the ever-present wind.
The dogwood's aflame. The big leaf maple's
right behind her. Lots of things

could easily ignite, which is why we dress you
in flame-retardant pajamas, circle your neck
with light-blue hearts.

The larkspur we waited for all summer
is finally blooming, but it's wrong—
bent beneath a cedar, snaking up,

snaking right back down. When your eyes are closed,
I focus on your eyelids. Your eyelids
and your breath, breath of the wind,

the cottonwood's applause. Because you open like a flower,
I leave a light on in the hall. Because each day
the red in the leaves a little redder,

I wish they were more like lullabies of unknown origin—
like the one you wake from to cake and pretty horses.
To explain them, I need to explain

country, God, passion, loyalty, love.
Because I don't know how else
to begin, I begin with love.

FOUR A.M.

Why is it the things you never think about at four in the afternoon
consume you at four a.m.? For instance why am I lying here just after the newspaper
bangs the front door asking myself how did I throw away all those letters
my mother's been sending

since college the ones telling me *sun's streaming temp near 40 may snow*
letters in which always a pot of soup is simmering *time to use up
old vegetables* hundreds of recipes Better than Ketchup

Acorn Squash Chili Tofu Sticks in long hand
with side notes *(cut sugar in half or substitute with cane juice)*
letters catching me up with family news *Uncle Willy's at a baseball conference*

in Pensacola Carol Anne's expecting her fourth Lottie's touring the West
letters *remind me to tell you the one about the cantaloupe
the potential wife needing to know the square root*

of minus one (dad told it better than me) letters
I might've easily stuffed in bags *wife & kids left him
at the peak of tree cutting season told her she had two choices:*

a parachute or a raft letters which did pile up
was it in my twenties? *Winston Sloan
put in a new lawn!* Even though

I was moving around a lot but then
I must've forgotten *how about some unshelled nuts
a see-through unbreakable container* how much I'd need her

gotta go brush teeth run out to look at a house just an idea driveway too steep
asking 159,000 forgot I'd ever be a mother my son
at four a.m. *Mama? Mama?* The letters I'll write him.

MY SON ASKS "WHAT'S A TORRENT?"

It's a womb, a swarm of worms, a swirling, untamed horn.
It's our bobbing, bubbling future, the dry leaf careening
beneath its branch as the first fat raindrops fall.

It's a gushing surging, riffling, swiftness; it's here,
where the river turns; there, where we heard the dipper
like water singing;

and now it's splashing, banging banks, swishing
past an overhanging willow like a girl with a comb
pulling and pulling her tangled hair.

Whole trees (it can happen; it happens) unleashing.
It's a swelling and bulging: the Skagit, the Sauk,
the Snoqualmie, the Stillaguamish. What the fishermen call

off color, an every-which-wayness all utterance (short
on restraint, hard to decipher), a violence purely, refreshingly
amoral, as in *Now I'll go this way, not that way*, cabins and coffins

loosening from comfortable clay. The mystery of mud stains
on three-story houses. Bursting, confusing, it could be
carrying your books, your wallet, your living room sofa;

it's friction's slurry and spin, the whole big, dark tugging
and gurgling jostle and sway of everything liquid,
our roiling, rapid-riding brains.

HIS FAVORITE COLOR IS GREEN

All shades all permutations
of say the shiny glabrous stem
of a shooting-out-from-winter daffodil
of Astroturf like just-before-blooming phlox

the long-&-narrow-little-or-large-town street sign
the big square Missoula Sioux City Throgsneck Bridge
along the freeway with horsetail astragalus vetch

the Libyan flag whipping over one point oh
three percent arable land
shimmer of mallard's head

or lighter . . . the under-ripe fruit
he does his best to enjoy
olivaceousness of kinglets
mama calliope warming her eggs
those clusters that fall in April or May
from Norway maples onto sidewalks
we stroller past
custard of scooped out avocado

or dark as say its skin . . . seaweed hemlock
dinosaur kale . . . picnic tables of city parks

The vegetables he hates
The garbage trucks he loves

The semi-spicate the glume-ful the spikelike the membranous
The shallowly bifid the twisted the sticky the hollow

The most common & palatable known
from near Corvallis from near Boise
Whorlwort Beckmannia False Brome

His world's frondy
Maidenhair gone haywire
His world's licorice wet (also deer & lady)
His world's hickory buckeye slippery elm

I kneel to find him something emerald
something emerald & squiggly

I hardly knew him that first spring he fit in a playground swing
ratcheting a metal bar along a chain
down & down till it fit

So much of his world so much of this world
even where plowed where fires even in cities
a hispid persistence

I wanted him to come along but he wouldn't
I wanted him to hurry
I needed to tell him what Horace said
about the goddess Envy
("leave no offerings")

Piles of clippings giant piles of invasive ivy
the neighbor's ghost-shaped shrubs harmless giants
while he sings his crocodile song

FORGETFULNESS THE GREAT BRONCHIAL TREE FROM WHICH I'M SWINGING

Forgetfulness the great bronchial tree from which I'm swinging
        nimble as a baby gorilla clenched fists slipping
through the farthest branch
        forgetfulness engaging my trapezius
reaching for what's inside my I thought safely guarded
        box of bones where I can't retrieve the word
for the thing in which I'm soaking
        forgetfulness falling to the back of the throat
back there with the uvula with the fauces
        not exactly the tip of the tongue more like the sublingual duct
my keys in the yard with the soupy tomatoes
        with the weepy zucchini
over the fence pecking seed
        forgetfulness the great Volkmann's canal
from which each day I hop a water taxi
        that deep and bony dentin
though forgetfulness too in the ever-eroding
        enamel the interstitial spaces my thoughts deciduous
teeth all eruption and loss oh these ossified
        ossificiations my husband's groaning
you forget everything epiglottis glotted
        fed-up-ness swelling his Adam's apple
proof of insurance recipe for *oeufs a la neige*
        a Ho Jo's in Far Rockaway
which keeps on calling
        claims I spent the night
aqueous fluids rushing the scene *Impossible!*
        my vitreous body holding firmly giving light

it's just I'm not sure I paid the mortgage
>plexus of *meant to should've not again!* Limbic system
lesioned? just the woman on the other end
>*says here you checked in 9/19*

LOW TIDE WALK WITH MARY GRACE

Even when it was low the water so far out it seemed it would never
Mary Grace her gum boots beige pants *high tide!* and we all ran
toward the road then *low tide!* and we all ran toward

the like I said impossibly far and the red sea nettle
don't touch though I doubt it was even alive
more about the not-moving-or-poking

concept though not exactly explicitly stated on principle
like the guy who carried the crab fifty yards from its home
by the big barnacled rock *take it back exactly*

which I'm not sure he regretted but as he carefully
Mary Grace looking on I was teaching my son
how to loosen rocks from sand the scrambling

and squirting the splashing not discouraging quite enough
the need to hold to keep to hurt my allegiance
to women like Mary Grace to the barnacle-

munching whelks the prehistoric isopods this frenzy of feeding
that comes and goes that came and went where now
these rocks and pools this warm green lace

THE FORBIDDEN FRUIT

was probably an apricot
but is almost always depicted

as shiny and red, the tree
the barren woman's supposed

to roll around beneath,
wash her hands with its juice.

How like us to choose,
for our eye-opening snack,

the one that hybridizes
with any other *Malus*, so that

planting a seed from a small and sour
might well yield a large and sweet.

"A good year for apples,
a good year for twins,"

The Dictionary of Superstitions said,
though weren't we glad when it turned out

not to be true. At the turn of the century,
Tobias Miller brought to Gold Hill, Oregon,

the King, the Northern Spy, the Yellow Transparent,
the Gravenstein, and the Greening,

though we're not sure what we're gathering—
stripey reds we peel and core for sauce,

yellows blushing in the summer sun.
When they ate of it, it tasted good,

twice as good, as say, eternity,
which could not be folded into cake,

which could not be put up or pressed.

AMANITA CALYPTRATA

The way we enter this world—an egg, a growing stalk,
a body sheathed in cottony white. The way we, too, emerge—

swathed in waxy vernix, sometimes still partially cloaked
in our amniotic sac, our sturdy homes like this universal veil,

not quite ready to let us go. This was what I was thinking
the first time I spotted, in the rapidly dampening woods,

Amanita calyptrata, the fall rains forging a river down our dusty drive.
Mushrooms Demystified likened them to *rare and secretive birds, a sunrise forming,*

a blanket of clouds, but to me they seemed oddly familiar, not unlike
what went on in millions of female bodies, not unlike what had happened

more than once in the womb of this 92-year-old now pointing to the picture,
asking me to confirm the dull-orange cap, cream-colored gills, fishy scent.

And who would have the nerve to doubt her, this woman who told me
over a meal of her own Chinook of her early attempts at landing fish

at the mouths of these local creeks, back in the 1930s? So, tonight I'm eating
Amanita, for how can I, how could anyone, pipe up with a *sorry I'm passing*?

Like passing up, despite the risks, the chance to raft this raging Rogue,
like turning tail, for no good reason, on your own expanding

womb, though you have to admit you're not quite up for an icy dousing,
though the memory of the group who mistook a related bunch

for straw mushrooms, not *phalloide*s, remains especially sharp.
In the end all your confidence will amount to less, much less,

than this pile of caps and stalks beside the sink—sleeplessness,
anxiety, estrogen's rapid decline—but off you go on your own raft,

Clonazepam and a baby nurse your two sworn antidotes. Off you go
to face whatever upset, whatever peril, this blessed bounty brings.

BEGGING TO DIFFER

*You had no choice but to ... join our joy, to dance
into my belly and rest / untroubled for 9 lovely months ...*
    ~ Laurie Albanese, *Our Bundle of Joy*

Fat, fucking hooey. Big, fat hunk of hulking, honking.
Hefty up heaved hunk right from those first aversions

to coffee, tomatoes, couscous, feta, anything served
more than once. *Joining our joy?* I might, just might, buy that—

joy of the day we conceived, or at least I think we conceived,
then hiked to Kelsey Creek where we watched

salmon pool up just below jagged boulders.
Skittish. Skid addling as we approached.

So unlike the sperm surrounding the egg,
breaking down the barriers that would soon

become our so-called dancing girl. But first bring on
the nosebleeds and the heartburn, the migraines

requiring codeine, bring on the nausea, that 6-month
stiff neck, waiting for results from the 2-in-100-causes-

miscarriage Chorionic Villous Sampling. Bring on the ultra-
sensitive ultrasounds (to screen out missing fingers, toes),

bring on the little dotted lines like vectors sashaying
along the screen, the carefully measured kidneys, lungs, tibias,

heart. Hooey altogether to *lovely*, our joy by now
the size of a no-see-um, opposite of joy

as I'm cocooned inside plastic for an MRI
(*we need to rule out aneurysm*). Hooey to any

would-be mom who says a fetus *rests*—
mine jolted me from sleep, bore down

till I puked—puked up not only juice
and crackers but water, plain water.

She didn't dance; she galloped. She didn't
do-si-do, hokey-pokey, or hullabaloo;

unhaltingly, she hammered; didn't divide
but devoured. The cosmos dances,

but an embryo? I see her more
as taking up shop, blow torch in one hand,

jack hammer in the other. Constantly flailing
two feisty fists. Making much more

than whirlpools in her mini-Jacuzzi.
It wasn't my womb to begin with.

Surely, those nine-some months, it was hers
and hers alone, till she got too big

to make her turns, to run her rumbling rudders,
till it was time for her to make her raucous, ruby-red debut.

I CAN'T WRITE

about her birth—about the way, when finally, after an eternity
of curling in and screaming, they plopped her on my chest

like a hot, wet seal, like something straight out of a warm
long-ago ocean, something slippery and covered with fur—

but I can write about the clock and its second hand,
how I gauged my progress by its slow and gentle circling

while I bounced on a blue ball, brought my cervix inch by inch
to ten. But I can't write, exactly, about dilation—how I stayed at three

till long past twelve, how progression didn't really begin
till after the almost-full moon had risen high enough to view it,

if we'd wanted, from that 5th floor brimming, overbrimming, with moaning
or pacing, passing again and again that giant yellow and red mangle

of a Deborah Butterfield horse, where instead we occupied ourselves
with ice water, heat packs, string cheese, spray from a Jacuzzi's jets—

or the number of times I pushed, but I can tell you that later that morning,
from three mini-blinded windows, I could hear the voices of children,

of mothers telling them to settle down, how I wished my womb, like theirs
(I presumed) had returned to the size of a fist. And I can tell you about

my bed, how I could lower it, how I could make it rise like a chair,
a ready-made chair for nursing, how in that bed I wished my daughter

were older than half a day, where both of us smelled not only of yeast
but of the acrid, earthiness of colostrum, of colostrum and vernix

and blood. I can't write about the lighting or give you anything close
to a time frame, but two of the nurses were named Sharon

and each of them told me, as I begged for an epidural,
you don't need one, *this is your birth and this is your labor, feel that* (the long

wait begun in late July nearly up). I wanted to keep detailed notes
about hazardous waste dispensers, my first try at aspirating

my baby's nose, about the breakfast of Cheerios and tea and French toast,
but instead these loosely woven undies one of the Sharons dubbed

"Madonna lingerie"—wear and toss—instead, the doula and my husband
walking me to the bathroom to get those panties on and off.

And I can tell you about the luxury, on a Friday night, of popping
two Ibuprofens, taking my first unfettered, unfetused shower in months,

but I can't remember much about that art on the third floor
where they made me walk and walk. All I can see is a cow

in the middle of a stream, on either side of her that blurry green of spring,
and two blue doors, one marked THE TRUTH, the other, EVERYTHING BUT.

WHAT LITTLE GIRLS ARE MADE OF

Tapir, pure tapir—all wide,
delicious ass. Herbivorous

to the core, union of fly rod
and shad roe. After hiking all the way up,

then all the way back down Mount Kinabalu.
In the month of pastels, fluorescent pink grass.

As American as a forest fire enveloping
your god-given home on the range.

With wheat berry eyebrows, resides
in the batter of Proust's madeline.

Also of the sorrowful women of Durer.
Of cantaloupe rind, of gargantuan zucchini.

Of Athena—all brains from the get-go, over-
brimming, teeming, full of knowing

hare-bell from bluebell, every genus
and every species, all brushed up

on conifer know-how, reminding us
spruces have papery cones.

Of granite, with meteor shower
skin, her nose, when it sniffs,

pre- and just- rainfall, her voice
a synthesis of Ginsberg and Plath—

"A Supermarket in London," amalgam
of nasty boy love and honey,

Lorca chasing her down the aisles hissing
Bees! You must devote yourself to bees!

"Babies in the tomatoes," yes,
but also of baby tomatoes. Of those believing

the world held up by a turtle. She's
the Thinker, Ye Olde Tick Tock.

She's the patch of geraniums
in full throttle, all wrists and sucking fists.

She's what glows and glows.

VICTORIA'S SECRET

's no secret, only rolls and saddles, only handles, gravity
doing as gravity does. I know this because after sifting

through piles of 36 Cs and 38 double D's—the pink & frilly, the dark & shiny—
all I can tell you is so much snappable spandex, so much Lycra,

cups twisted like handcuffs in countries where no one speaks
of the right to remain silent. If there's a secret, it's lost on me, unless

it's knowing, if you need assistance, you can push a button,
& a woman will enter your room saying she's built exactly like you—

not full-figured, but entitled to breasts like two stiff dollops
of whipped-up whites. Tell her to bring you what held up

the lunar module, all that jostling and bouncing.
Tell her maybe the secret's the stuff our galaxy's

been dishing up for eons, Newton's apples, what we've always
always known. Maybe we could all learn a few things

from Jupiter and Saturn, resembling, as they often do,
those glamorous, distant stars.

FROM

*THE LITTLE OFFICE OF THE
IMMACULATE CONCEPTION*

2011

MY PLACE IN THE UNIVERSE

I think I am here
to stare carefully at maps,

then get lost at least fifty times a year.
I think I am here

to be suddenly
made aware of the loudness

of a ticking clock,
also to witness, in unexpected places,

glitter,
to hear a lady in heels

walking assertively down a hall.
The universe and I,

we are both expanding our knowledge
of what's just beyond us.

Me-n-the universe
really not separate after all,

me surely not a subset.
Me, the chairs, all

the couches, every soda can,
every book and eyelash,

all together making a music
unfortunately no one can hear

on account of the humming exhaust fans,
on account of the humming lights.

I LIVE ON MILK STREET

Via Lactea, to be exact. Once it was the path
to Zeus's palace, then a creamy cul de sac; now

they just keep widening and widening. Its origin?
On that the jury's still out. It could have been paved

by the Holy People who crawled to the surface
through a hollow reed, then formed my kind

from ears of white and yellow corn. Some say
it was born of Juno's wrath, wrath that tore

her breast from a suckling infant Hercules
(her no-good hubby once again knocking up

a mortal). What spurted up, they tell me,
begat this little avenue, this broad and ample road

where I merry-go-round with my 200-300
billion neighbors, give or take a billion or two.

(Then again, it might've all been cooked up
by Raven.) My street has the mass

of a trillion suns; my roundabout's a black hole.
My backyard abuts with my dear friend Io's.

She's always asking me to come on over,
but enduring speeds upward of 106,000 mph

usually means I'm waving from the porch.
(On the plus side, the ash from her many volcanoes

does wonders for my whispering bells.) I do wish
I could get to know the Leptons, though.

I invite them to my cookouts, but they're off
to hither and yon. And I don't mean to be catty,

but it's high time Ms. Nuclear Bulge
ponied up for a some high power Spanx.

I know there's a whole lot else out there—
starbursts, whirlpools, magellanic clouds—

but I'm busy enough keeping up
with the slugs attacking my pole beans,

making sure the garbage goes out. Truth be told, I'm happy
right here where I am, lulled by my own sweet byway's

hazy halo, its harmony of traffic.

OURS

contains the ripping-metal croak
of a wader who eats its prey whole;
also a frog resembling a leaf, the male's
throat stuffed with its tadpole young;
we have tapeworms that latch
to intestinal walls, each segment self-
replicating. I guess we're all about making
more. And Styrofoam. And toilet paper.
We take pictures of empty parking lots
to show that sometimes they want us straight,
and sometimes they want us diagonal. Sculpt
from wood a human head, a headscarf
shrouding it, but stop me, I hardly know you.
         Okay, if you insist. We have pancreatic juices,
Extreme Shampoo for the dead cells shooting
from our non-wooden heads, and we have music,
magnetism, and dreams. We can drive forever
past nothing but wheat or corn, but then Mumbai,
22,000 people per square mile. Do you have
hobbies? Our favorite's folding paper into cranes;
we also love horses and wiping each other out.
Our creation myth? A pool of acid and sugar
walked into a cave, began to paint on walls.
Has anyone mentioned fear?
         Where am I going? *Crazy. Wanna come?*
as my mom used to say, which is replication; mostly,
as I've said, what we do. We believe in money,
random mutation, though greed screws up everything.
But that Calder in Michigan—*The Grand Vitesse?*—
that's the kind of upward mobility we all can relate to.

We pilate; we retreat, heal ulcers
with maggots; we nudist colony, vanilla
to Cozahome till wakened by a child's *who made
this world?* We'd like to be kissed and kissed
by a good kisser, touched and loved in a shade
of lipstick that becomes us. Invent new names
for cities and birds. To carry our young like a leaf-
like frog. Our world is an oven; we are the temperature.

WHAT I WILL TELL THE ALIENS

I will tell them about our clapping,
our odometers, and our skillets.

I will take them to a place of fierce
lightning, to a place of tombstones

and of gridlock, and I will tell them
of geckos, of ecstatic moments,

all about our tchotchkes, our temples,
our granite-countered kitchens.

Give me an alien and I will give it
a story of unfathomable odds,

of erections and looting. Show me
an alien and I will show it the sorrows

of the centuries, all wrapped up
in a kerchief, all wrapped up

in a grandmother's black wool coat.
Bring me an alien right now,

and I will show it the misery
of stilettos, of pounding out

tortillas and gyros. Please—
send me an alien, and I will give it

a bloody nose, and then I will show it a great
humanitarian gesture, 10,000 tents

when 600,000 are needed. Let me
talk to these aliens about shoe-shiners

and rapture, of holidays and faxes;
let me pray with the aliens for the ice

to stop melting, for the growths to stop
growing, for a gleam to remain on our lips

long after the last greasy French fry is gone.

IN PRAISE OF NOT GETTING

What time is it when an elephant sits on a fence?
Time for the chicken to wander lonely as a road, time

for the full-fledged conniption fit about what's not
on the fence or the road—*not that pink one! The other*

pink one! The one with the blue balloon on its rump,
the one she's grown fond of, used to, the one to grow on,

grown on, drone on, which is what time it is, and what makes it
so special? And he says sparkles, but I say a story I can't quite

figure out. I say, we need a verb: to art! To take the ho hum mundane,
and sparkle-ize it. Catch my glittery drift? Mine glimmering eye?

As in degree of usefulness. As in what the eye wants. Like billboards
salivating the dollar burger. Yes, we laughed when we saw the one

about the unibrow, but then we bought the ticket, bought it like the functions
of light and dark—sun equals crops, darkness tucks us into bed—

vs. all things good and bad. And also it's tidying. Sensing there's a mess,
making sense of it. Assemblage. Installation. Here, let me

untangle that. There, I unraveled the ball of yarn that guy's
been twining since 1967. Hiring a maid, a ready-made.

Half the time de-conundruming, the other half
upping the chaos, making the messes, messes of messes,

going, you call that a storm? I'll show you a storm, blasting
the viewer to Neptune's 900-mile-an-hour winds. Riddling the regular

with reindeer rivets. Oh, and better make sure it strikes a chord
any Hindu, hay-seed, or Yoruba can grok (grok that?).

But really it's just arranging, an arrangement, a bunch
of peonies, a couple irises, six long-stemmed roses. Not cut

and dried ones; real ones you put in water. Ungraspable's
good, too, as in stung like stinging nettle. As in this could be

a dream of eating ants, or this could be eating ants. But how,
you ask, did the Brillo pad scrub its way into a museum

my three-year-old could've built? Read above, where I mention
billboards, degree. What does art guide or guard? A whisper

of irony, a poke at documentary veracity, absurdity you may
or may not catch. I should hope it welcomes spies in the house

of serendipity, the calling into question of everything hanging
on every gallery's walls, but that's just my Jackson Pollock splatting.

And then there's wanting to crack the safe, break into that box
because tick-tock the game is locked. As in let me see, am I

seeing this right? It's a pill, isn't it? An insect eye? A sort of button
to push? A microcosm? A spaceship, no, yes, one of the 1,500

galaxies in Deep Field North? I knew it! I just knew it! A fertility goddess
walking her dog! Something that used to happen freely (freedom?)

that's recently been fenced. Something like feedlot confinement, I bet.
Or, no: I know! A subdivision, plans for the Fidalgo Bay Expansion,

complete with where the water will go. A trilobite? Or. She'd had
an identity and lost it. Her identity now orbiting like that 28,000-

km-per-hour glove dropped by a Gemini astronaut, the most dangerous
garment in history. Art is a dangerous garment. Art is a dress you don't

wear to work. Art's best kept with the cowboy poetry boots and the atheist-
patterned tights. Don't want to get art on your face, either. It might

make your neighbor edgy, especially if you ask him to share his thoughts
about the imagination. Discuss, instead, mowers, whether to go

with gas or electric. Ask to borrow his edger. Ask if it's time
your lawn had more edge. Or. She'd never been one for solving riddles,

but she liked a good joke. And fences make good neighbors.

ODE TO IMAGINATION

and image, Vostok 1 hurling Yuri Gagarin
200 miles above us, what the optic nerve's

efforant fibers unstitch, then carry its post-
orbit parachuting news to the retina. News

the earth is blue, so we look and when we do
our brain's not calling up a replica from its cache

of Polaroids stuffed in an attic drawer,
but a brand new view of *vortex, tundra, crashed*,

of John Glenn's capsule, with John Glenn inside!
At the point of re-entry, his tin-can home sustaining

quadruple-digit temps. How are you imagining it?
I'm seeing half a dozen loafered, skinny-tied guys

cozied around a computer the size of the Gorge
in George, Glenn, squeezed in, bolted-up, triple-checking

Friendship's gauges. Fragile, fragile like an eggshell,
a cool, crisp morning in August. And Glenn,

not much good at *like* or *as*, with no *small steps*
or *giant leaps* up his space-suited sleeve *the sky*

in space is very black. This moment of twilight
is very beautiful . . . Okay, so we can't all be Keats,

and besides, could a *scop* have stood the stress of a strap
from the retropackage swinging around, fluttering

past the capsule window? Would you've preferred
the poet-astronaut spurting metaphors as the smoking

apparatus ignites? Glenn kept his white-knuckled wits,
and the rest is Apollo 11, the ghost drum ungoblined,

the silent victory trumpet triumphant, a halo go round
the moon. But back to Gagarin, the flash and the dark,

back to the viewer taking it in *Mama, wanna see, wanna see?*
Mama, you're not looking! Mama lifting off in her Cosmodrome,

to a place where image meets interference, life
by a thousand shadows, the interplay between brain

and eye working overtime to lift us off this earth.

THE LITTLE OFFICE OF THE IMMACULATE CONCEPTION

is almost always closed. More good news: no place
to kneel, no place to leave off applications,
though also no place for asking *how in the world?*

Hail, Queen Spermicide Dodger! Hail, Mistress
of the Quicker than Quickie! Hail, nothing close
to a virgin, of the messy-as-all-get-out birth!

Soiled diaper of the morning, shit enshrin'd!
O half-pint half drank, make speed to the help
of humankind. O my quiver, my queen of puppies,

mother of all goats and one purple unicorn. Mistress
of the aphid, who forsakest no one and despiseth no one
(except her brother, mostly when he swipes—except

her brother, when he swipes). Look upon me
with an eye of pity, o gherkin who'll soon be grown,
for I am the one who washes thy blueberry-stained bibs,

who droppeth to her knees to wipe up the milk
and the meat. Celebrate with devout affection
thine holy and immaculate conception, which by the way

is actually the story of bypassing a dousing
of Non-Oxynol 9. So, hereafter, by the grace
of Him whom thou, liveth and reigneth in perfect

purple and orange plaid skort. Hail, munchkin
most moist! Hail, seven furry caterpillars, the table
scribbled with brown and blue ink. Hail, new word: ant.

O perpetual snot! O paperclip in your mouth!
O gate you're stuck behind (with good reason)!
O lost marbles! O pure arc from changing table

to bathtub, fair rainbow of stench. Hail and dwell
in the highest, hail purity, which lasts about two seconds.
My lily among bits of plaster, dying parsley, keeling over

kale, spent tomatoes. Thanks to you, dear bombardier,
I'm the mother of mercy. Thanks to you I give hope
to the guilty. You with your three pink blankets,

you with your avocado smears, you drooling olives.
Me with my need to straighten, my need for quiet,
right here in this little office, this little

immaculate office, where a healthy glob
of pharmaceutical this-and-that couldn't stop you.
O rage! O sperm! O last of my healthy eggs!

Here where we cooked you up
like a cherry-almond tart—cinnamon, flour, butter
(1 ¼ cold unsalted sticks). Coarse crumbs worked

to a ball. Let us pray, holy girl, though not
in martyrdom's palm; let us pray, enthralled.

AFTER READING THERE MIGHT BE AN INFINITE NUMBER OF DIMENSIONS

I'm thinking today of how we hold it together,
arrive on time with the bottle of Zinfandel, a six-pack

of Scuttlebutt beer, how we cover our wrinkles
with Visual Lift, shove the mashed winter squash

into the baby's mouth, how we hold it all together
despite clogged rain gutters, cracked

transmissions, a new explanation for gravity's
half-hearted hold. I'm wondering how we do it,

comb the tangles from our hair, trim the unwieldy
lavender, speak to packed crowds about weight loss

or fractals. I'm wondering how we don't
fall to our knees, knowing a hardened pea,

lodged in the throat, can kill, knowing
liquids are banned on all commercial flights.

Leaves fall. The baby sucks her middle fingers.
Meanwhile, the refrigerator acquires

an unexplainable leak. Meanwhile, we call
the plumber, open wide for the dental hygienist,

check each month, with tentative circlings,
our aging breasts. Somehow, each morning,

the coffee gets made. Somehow, each evening,
the crossing guard lifts her fluorescent orange flag,

and a child and her father cross the glistening street.

POOR BANISHED CHILDREN OF EVE

I believe in the dish in the sink
not bickering about the dish in the sink
though I believe the creator

of the mess in the living room
cleans up the mess in the living room
sucks up cracker pizza potpie peanut popcorn

and I believe in the earth which also ends up on the rug
which must also be vacuumed up as I acknowledge
our blessings running water not teeming with toxins

and even though this might sound like nagging
especially in the face of dying and of burial
and of purgatory and of hell especially when

I could be instead of asking could you please
wipe up the olive juice that little pile of parsley
wailing and moaning at your wake

or maybe just sitting there stunned where beside me
sitteth the six year old and the 19-month-old who most definitely
wouldn't get the dying concept though maybe the son

from thence being the owner of two dozen dead ladybugs
And I believe in the holy in the hole in the toe
of his feet-in pajamas *Mama look how much I grew*

in just one night! His reminder I own a sewing kit
and also all the holy saints (especially the martyrs)
the resurrection of peace-sign pasta three nights running

and the father of course thy will be done
though in fact a whole lot doesn't get done
like fixing the cracked windows re-upping prescriptions

or dusting let's not forget dusting hallowed be the trip
to Safeway for lettuce yogurt our daily beer
and lead us away from bitching about picking up

the hallowed son from the bus stop
lead us away from resenting the filing
the trips to the curb to the bank

lead us away from martyrdom
(though did we mention we love the saints)
lead us away from the temptation to chuck it all flee

to Thetis Island and glory be to dishwashing liquid
and the sponge glory to the microwave and Mr. Coffee
for the world and all its Huggies all its wet wipes

glory be and have mercy and save us from the pot
of boiling water from the fires otherwise known
as letting the smoke-alarm battery go dead

to thee do we cry poor banished children of Eve
poor ants at the mercy of unforeseen disaster
poor praying mantises stuck in our plastic cages

poor and thankless a valley of tears
though actually a giant crevasse
grant us eternal grant us merciful
o clement o loving o sweet

LOVE
> *with apologies to Julie Sheehan*

I hate your kneecaps floating free
in their salty baths. I hate your knees,

both of them, and I hate your eyelashes,
especially the ones that fall out, the ones

you're supposed to wish on; I wish you
bad wishes. I hate every hair

on your hairy face, hate you as much
as I hate being put on hold,

thank you for your patience
when I have none, when patience

is as far away as my first grade teacher's
if you have nothing nice to say . . .

Your mushroom risotto: hate it.
The salmon you're defrosting: hate.

My vowels hate you.
My adverbs hate you. The backyard

hates you—the backyard with all its abandoned
dump trucks, with the giant hole our son dug

all summer while soaker hoses soaked. That hole
and all holes, including the hole in the ozone,

which of course keeps growing bigger.
Spaghetti wrapping around a fork.

Mashed spinach and carrots caught
in the rungs of a high chair, stuck

to the floor like dried green paint: hate,
hate, hate. Each furry rabbit a little furry ball

of hate. Each blackberry a messy drupe of drippy hate.
At the China Palace the plates piled high with Mu Shu

Hate, the plates now a busboy's burden of hate,
the only sound the dumpster's clanging *hate hate hate.*

THIS PARENTING THING

which I love which I hate
the love part easy not torture at all

like his asking *spell furniture* while we wait
outside the Rogue River Fly Shop

like checking to see if the faeries came
his digging with a blue shovel while I weed

the broccoli the kale and even asking
over and over for a gummy worm

which I will not give him he's already
had three and that's just the beginning

the first few words of the brook
that flashes and foams that keeps on

with its garter-snake awe with its ant fascination
all of it not yet drooped not yet fallen in a heap

till all that's left is a rose hip
a hip you could dry and make a tea with

but will you? But that's the least of it
barfing croup a temperature of 105

the day he mistook motor oil for bubble bath
the day he ate the insect repellant *just be lucky*

they're healthy how dare you hate his sneakiness
his thrown-out crusts just be lucky you don't live

in Nigeria where polio's making a comeback
just be glad you don't live nearly anywhere else

but what about my one-year-old her three or four
or sometimes fifteen nighttime feedings

can I hate what sleeplessness does to a brain
like I'm caught in amber whenever

multi-cellular beings formed
dragging along reaching for sugar caffeine

like some ammonite some primitive mollusk
a little closer I'll admit to all that lives

but not quite sane when she starts to choke
on a piece of grocery list the firemen storming

where is she? to de-lodge the marble or dime
to turn her upside down and whack her

till the bead or pebble slips out
though by the time they arrive

I've pulled out the guilty party and she's cooing
Love it? Love it? Yep yep especially

the notes that come from school
Riley helped a sad friend today

or looking up to see in place of her face
a lime green plastic plate anticipating

my *peek-a-boo!* though could live without
the half-way through yoga right when we're about

to start on shoulder stands *I think she wants
her mama* though bet you'd find it hard to believe

feeding her mashed peas and rice I'm already
longing for the silver and turquoise spoon

for what falls to her sleeve but then she's screaming
and I'm screaming over her screaming

carrying on the conversation hating
what she takes longing for evening's relief

though longing too for morning though dreading the bib
and the apple sauce wriggling her into pink plush jeans

though not wanting her anywhere close
to asking for keys and meanwhile my son

can't stop asking where is it who has it
and all about the kid who owns it now

forever and ever until he discovers there's one with spots
and that one will do which lasts about fifteen minutes

my whole life snatched away for procurement forms
for reading him *Goodnight Moon* and *Click, Clack, Moo*

for lifting her up to the doctor's scale
watching the numbers line up

MORE WAVES MAY FOLLOW

I told her *your hair has lovely waves*
so she waved like the white-gloved

Miss Merry Christmas on the Christmas float.
He said *my egg beater runned out of gas* because

it was his mower, the same one his father used
to keep the house from burning down. We do not

anticipate this, but if tables and chairs
begin to fall over, do not expect

another warning. When he heard me say
proscuttio he thought *pro-shoot-o*, so the tongs

a new kind of power, a weapon all his own.
Begin to fall over our only warning; there was no other.

I wish I could die he'd said so now he had his chance
(now I was surely listening). And I'd said

nothing negative (we were talking
about subtraction, how you can't take

four away from two), but this has nothing to do
with positive. They were expecting me

to save them, and that was a little jarring,
especially when I looked up Third Street, knew

it was floating with bodies. Do not pack
your belongings; don't recount your longings.

Every wrong thing you did had a reason.
She's running from me, won't let me

comb her hair; he wants to lie down
in the road, let the rushing run him over.

We are the waves. We are the numbers.
We are *no one's watching over us*

and *this is just what happens.*
We are the sinking, yet all the while

*we can go to another world—all we need to do
is doggy paddle*—our insurance, her hair ties,

his haiku with the springing deer—
all in a churn, our stay at the hotel

over, our only warning the falling.

HOW TO SEW

You need a mouthful of pins.
You need a Simplicity pattern,

the onion-skin sheets explaining—
with dotted lines, with numbers
and arrows—palazzo pants, a hooded dress.

The best part is the storeowner,
her rhinestone pince-nez glasses,

how she flips and flips your chosen bolt,
lavender fabric spilling out
like a colossal ribbon candy.

The best part is the sound of scissors
slicing through a poly-cotton blend.

You will need to learn
about edges, about gathers.

Meanwhile, the whole contraption
disguised to look like a table. Meanwhile,

lifting the lid, reaching in
for the smooth black cat, needle

for a mouth. Meanwhile, threading
the bobbin; the squeaking

of the foot pedal. You will discover
there is satisfaction in edgestitching.
Edgestitching and stitch ripping.

You will wear the flawed apron,
but only you will know the flaw.

You will learn to tie off knots.

EASTER VISIT

Her poofy pink dress had a hole in it long before Jesus staged
His annual comeback, her Mary Jane's brown with Ozark mud

before there was even a rumor of rising. The plastic egg grandma would find
on her lawn next week hadn't yet been filled with a rubbery squid.

Her daughter/their mother had fallen behind, hadn't yet made the trek
for Peeps, fluorescent grass, hadn't rustled down the pig for Sunday brunch.

But soon the eggs hidden, the soccer ball basket, the bunny basket stuffed
inside a prickly bush, and soon enough they're running for the plastic lamb

barely resembling a lamb, for colors non-existent except at Wal-Mart,
soon enough all or nearly all, scooped up, added to the pile, and they're off

to the Salvation Army church, where the boy playing lead guitar
is cousin Carmen, the kid transformed to a turquoise-bunny-eared

rock star. *Through the veil of gloom and darkness / Where o death is now thy sting?*
Uncle Matt's triumphant percussion, Aunt Christi's booming, blessed soprano,

Rosie the soldier waving her hands, holding up God's ceiling, marching
as she sings. And then they're out of there, the kids with their bubble wands

and wind-up chicks, with their new, vague sense of a long-haired, bearded,
sheet-swathed, half-naked guy encircled in beams of light and clouds,

the daughter trying out a *hallelujah* in the backseat scattered
with 250 million year old gastropod fossils now headed

for the sanctuary of the dirt road, for a forest resplendent
with mayapple, wake-robin, bloodroot, and the kids, itchy and hot,

too hot for clothes, peel them off, squeal through the just-leafed
dogwoods, hickories, sycamores, oaks, their voices lifting with each

squirrel, each unfurling fern. Full and hot, as if they'll never be hungry,
never be cold again, as if this forest's party dress will never tatter;

biscuit-glutted, resurrection-drunk in the Oklahoma heat, cardinals
exploding *Who-it? Who-it? Who-it?* Rosie cautioned not to heed

the anthems of the dead—Buddha, Allah, Krishna (*Ours is the only one
who rose*), to stay for Bible Study, to trade in coos and croaks, buzzes

and chirps for Matthew 28, all the while every spring beauty, each
poking-from-the-duff morel: *we're back, we're back; we've come back to life.*

IT'S ALL GRAVY

a gravy with little brown specks
a gravy from the juices in a pan

the pan you could have dumped in the sink
now a carnival of flavor waiting to be scraped

loosened with splashes of milk of water of wine
let it cook let it thicken let it be spooned or poured

over bird over bovine over swine
the gravy of the cosmos bubbling

beside the resting now lifted to the table
gravy like an ongoing conversation

Uncle Benny's pork-pie hat
a child's peculiar way of saying *emergency*

seamlessly   with sides of potato of carrot of corn
seamlessly   while each door handle sings its own song

while giant cicadas ricochet off cycads and jellyfish sting
a gravy like the ether they swore the planets swam through

luminiferous   millions of times less dense than air
ubiquitous   impossible to define   a gravy like the God

Newton paid respect to when he argued
that to keep it all in balance to keep it from collapsing

to keep all the stars and planets from colliding
sometimes He had to intervene

a benevolent meddling like the hand
that stirs and stirs as the liquid steams

obvious and simple   everything and nothing
my gravy your gravy our gravy   the cosmological constant's

glutinous gravy   an iridescent and variably pulsing gravy
the gravy of implosion   a dying-that-births-dueodenoms gravy

gravy of doulas of dictionaries and of gold
the hand stirs   the liquid steams

and we heap the groaning platter with glistening
the celestial chef looking on as we lift our plates

lick them like a cat come back from a heavenly spin
because there is oxygen in our blood

because there is calcium in our bones
because all of us were cooked

in the gleaming Viking range
of the stars

FROM

RECKLESS LOVELY

(2014)

PALE BLUE DOT

Candice Hansen-Koharcheck, I'm not sure how
to pronounce your name, but you were the first

to spot it, this two-pixel speck otherwise known
as Earth. Sitting at your screen, shades drawn,

office dark, you searched the digital photos sent back
by Voyager 1, four billion miles from your desk.

And there it was, not the big blue marble swirling
with clouds and continents, not the one Apollo astronauts

the sheer beauty brought tears—thanking God and America,
declaring no need to fight over borders or oil. This was not

that view. This was how our planet might look to an alien.
And yet how close this photo came to not being taken at all.

Scientists arguing aiming the camera back at the sun
might fry the lens, questioning the worth of such a risk.

This shot you say still gives you chills, dear Candice,
our planet bathed in the spacecraft's reflective light.

Pale blue dot lit by a glowing beam: I'm surprised
Christians didn't have a heyday, though viewing

His crowning achievement requires squinting.
When NASA put it on display at the Jet Propulsion Lab,

a blow-up print spanning fourteen feet, visitors touched
the pinprick so often the image needed constant replacing,

perhaps because without the little arrow we wouldn't know
which pinprick was home. And yet its barely-there-ness

doesn't excuse the plastic bags, duct tape, juice packs,
and sweatpants that lodge in the stomachs of whales. And yet

its lack of distinction doesn't pardon the brown-pudding goop
on the Gulf of Mexico's floor, a goop in which nothing alive

has been found. To reckon that speck, mourn the loss
of the black torrent toad. To take it in, grasp its full weight,

then turn toward a child's insistent *give me a ride in a rocket ship!
With meteors and turbulence!* Like you, dear Candice, alone

and in the dark while a loved one's asking
Where are you going? When are you coming back?

LA GIOCONDA

I'm deaf, I'm in mourning; I've just had a 2nd child.
I'm toothless, palsied, pregnant, paralyzed.

Clearly, I'm a reflection of the painter's neuroses;
clearly, I have a toothache. Turn the canvas

sideways, at a 45-degree angle. Scan the dark swirls:
and you'll see them, the buffalo and the lion. Twenty

animals in all, including a snake representing
envy, a leopard because its skin kills the wanting

of what we don't have. I'm the Jolly Lady, wife
of Francesco del Giocondo; I'm Lisa (a real-life person);

I'm idealized, the artist's mother, the Madonna (a mule
nestles between my breasts—have you spotted

the ape?) Superimposed on a Chinese landscape,
I'm the eternal female, queen of sepulchral secrets.

My half-smile is the smile of enlightenment,
and those glowing hands? So Buddha. In 1962,

posing with Jackie and JFK, I was valued at $720 million,
six times the price of a Pollock or de Kooning.

Some have said that in my placid eyes tiny letters
and numbers reveal I'm Gian Giamono Caprotti,

my painter's apprentice, but don't buy it.
Forget the theories relating to my lack

of eyebrows and lashes, lost not from plucking
but the ravages of restoration. Housed at Versailles,

entwined myself in the Sun King's cucumber patch,
silently basked in Les Tuileries while Napoleon, quaffing

his coveted Chambertin, scuffed around in beat-up red slippers.
When WW2 broke out, they wrapped me in waterproof paper,

whisked me to a land of poppies and castles. Behind
two layers of bulletproof glass, I live on at the Louvre,

where each year seven million spend an average
of fifteen seconds discerning my ambiguous mood. I'm

unfinished; I've been stuffed beneath a trench coat, smuggled
back to Florence. Doused with acid, stoned, pummeled

with a teacup. Touched-up, varnished, de-varnished, infested
with insects; fumigated. I'm a miasma of optical illusions;

my paint is cracking. My visage excites the random noise
in your visual system; emotion recognition software reveals

I'm 83% happy, 9% disgusted, 6% fearful, two pinches angry,
one iota neutral. You love me like you love your sphinx,

your flying saucers, your Area 51; I'm your koan,
your inscrutable floozy, your syphilitic conundrum,

your angelic aspara, your enduring durga. You're here
because I render you agog, aha-less, uncomfortably mum.

ODE TO FRIDA KAHLO'S EYEBROWS

Cult of the brow ascending like a condor,
of refusal to bow to the whimsy of busy tweezers.
From follicle to follicle, freedom unfurls.
Brow most buxom. Ferret brow.
Brow channeling Hieronymus Boschian shenanigans.
Brow championing Duchampian high jinx.
Brow side-skirting ye olde pot o wax.
Brow hobnobbing with Salvadori Dali's mustache.
Mink stole brow; brow I-stole-it-from-a-rodent.
Brow suggesting a profuse, gargantuan beard.
Circus-circuit brow.
Brow that never shook hands with laser.
Most inexplicable brow, most unpixelated.
Bad luck black kitten brow on the prowl.
Mercury in retrograde brow.
Brow undaunted by a John Deere tractor.
Brow the embodiment of national glory.
Brow the mystic mestiza, but brow also
weeping with dislodged fetus, with loss and forlornness.
Brow a come-hither furry viper.
Brow the little known Black Shag Slug.
Brow the unretractable bewhiskered tongue.
Brow the fleecy fluke, tufted cobra, downy leech.
Brow the dark secret of the fastidiously plucked,
that perpetual raised-brow surprise.
Brow surprising, but unsurprised.
Brow the prismatic lion in the wardrobe
when you were expecting beige scarves.
Brow adding a bristly flourish to bright Tehuana dress.

Sing holy praises to the insistence of the brow.
Sit down and write a letter to the core beliefs of the brow.
Knit a sweater to the milagro-like votivity of the brow.
Conjure new words to praise the liftingness of brow.
Flamenco to the mural-worthiness of the brow.
Praise god for the untamability of the brow.
Brow most steadfast. Brow on endless loop,
brow most perennial, most acanthus.
Brow aching yet soaring like an unruffled raven.
Unamputated brow.
Brow never renouncing its femininity.
Feminine brow donning its midnight suit.
Brow the corpse that proves the path to the next.
Brow never resting in peace.
Long live the flourish of the stalwart, seaward sooty gull in every self-portrait.
Long live the childlike exuberance of the feisty, the feral. Long live the monkeys
and parrots, perched beside the unwieldy, the emblematic.
Long live those wooly-bear wonders worthy of worship,
like two black wings—signature smudges left by the pig
twirling on a spit *todos los dias, todas las noches*.

SUMMONS AND PETITION FOR NAME CHANGE

Abelmosk. Abracadabra. Abruzzi. Absolute.
Bonzery. Bogan. Love's barometer. Bristly ballerina.
Choo-choo cherry sanctum. Cutie-cute caldera.
Dim sum-my dilberry. Down there Daiquiri.
Ear of Eden. Eminently Earthy. Empress Gensho.
Fandango-ing funnel. Fox foot. Flamingo.
Geranium in the Gate of the Gourd. Gentian's grin.
Hallelujah in the huckleberry. Ho-Ho-Kus.
Inner Inagaddadavida. Ink on the isthmus.
Jupiter's Big Red Spot. Un-January. Jambalaya.
Knit Kit. Kittewake. Kinnick-kinnick. Nether katzenjammer.
Laniferous lability. Hello Kitty lunch box. Lettuce cup asunder.
Mythic mouth. Mama's milk pan melts Emanuel. Maenadic moon.
Name It Not, Why Not? Nemorous nook. Nefertiti's niche.
O'Keeffe. Unfrozen o-ring. Open the sunroom window.
Persimmon portal. Passworded pomegranate. Paisy-waisy.
Quaint Quiver. Quaking qat. Unquashable squab.
Rorschach-y rivulets. Ragmatical raven. Electric rabbit.
Susquehanna. Multi-syllabic sizzler. So strawberry.
Too much fun. Tell me another. Tisket. Tasket. Trisket.
Umbilical's prologue. My own undeniable. Under my undies.
Velvet-it's-not. Venus vector. Victory garden. Vroom-vroom.
Webbed Wednesday. Whipped up elixir. Wowie. Wha-wha.
Xizang. Xebec. Anti-xeric. Excitable raptor. Fringy xenon.
Yeti. Yangtze. Ygdrasil. *Yucca whipplei.* Yokozuma. Yapese dime.
Zounds-mound. Spangled zarf. Naughty zloty. Zerk gone berserk.

WOLVES KEEP IN TOUCH BY HOWLING

and I keep in touch
with *you're pissing me off*

you're pushing my buttons
I'm not interested in rescheduling

Listen! Do you hear that?
That's my tongue licking

a laceration, a bloody metacarpal,
a fracture; that's my nasal baritone,

my *UUUUUU* unfurling your foothold.
Wolves keep in touch,

and I with my keen sense
sense extirpation (necrosis

suspected; necrosis likely). I scent;
I fang; I phalange; I from helicopters;

I for sport; I greedy chew my foot off;
I trickster; I snout. Wolves howl

in the smoothest of coats, guard hairs
shining, repelling the sopping.

Hackles raised, tail rigid, I'm fixing my stare
on the adamant, my ears to each leaf

as it falls.

LEONARDO DA VINCI'S GRAN CAVALLO

For seventeen years he sketched it,
made models from clay, built

a 20-meter-deep casting pit, devised
a system of temporized furnaces.

His medium? 70 tons of molten bronze
to be poured, in less than three minutes,

into the mold of a 24-foot horse.
This he'd been commissioned to do

by the Duke of Milan, in honor
of the Duke's father, Francesco,

though Francesco disappeared
from the horse's back early on,

the artist so wrapped up in equine-
osity, in forelocks and withers,

in coronets and hocks, in learning,
from bell makers, how best

to render a boisterous animal
rearing up unsaddled, unfettered,

unreined, though in the end the bronze
could not be melted into muzzle

or mane, though into the end,
in the Battle of Marignano,

the bronze he'd been promised
snatched away, hauled

through the Alps
as seventy cannons.

THE POET IS THE PRIEST OF THE INVISIBLE

~ Wallace Stevens

Dark-eyed, mysterious Meadowhawk,
the poet is the rabbi of the diaphanous,

scribe of the sheer, the barely-there
brief, pungi of the five o'clock shadow,

hint of rosewood and ghost. The poet
preaches a thin-barked willow sermon;

what she labors over is always prone
to sunscald, to scrutiny, its veins

visible through the skin. Gossamer
goddess, translucent muse, she lofts

a gauzy lug wrench toward the shadowy
freeway, where the alphabet—each of its

limpid clauses, each hyaline verb—
has once again broken down, needs a lift.

WHAT FALLS FROM TRUCKS, FROM THE LIPS OF SAVIORS

South of Cincinnati two thousand cotechini slipped from their crates
onto a rush-hour roadway, rain concocting a puke-red slush.

When sweeping proved futile, Jet Vacs rescued the route, funneling
drivers toward the Ohio, a drive now eerie with the ghosts of innards.

Others have crashed into guardrails, drifted toward the center lane,
dumped delicatas and lava, brought to their doom dozens of goats,

passels of pullets, let loose a long, mucilaginous swath of glue,
dinged medians with thirty tons of Idaho spuds, unleashed

twelve million bees. Between the Jordan River and Damascus,
along the Visa Maris, in the early first century AD, along

with a quarter ton of Sunkist navels, Jesus pelted the populace
with *thou shalt have no other*, knocking out all communication

with Sabazius, the practice of flogging with vipers, anointing
with bran and mud, which also put a swift halt to the cult

of Dionysus (tambourines clashing, goat guts bleating for mercy,
dripping blood bedabbled ...), cult of the dizzying Pharaoh's Fury,

Teacup Frenzy, of *he was not the God of libation – he was the libation.*
Sin washed up from the Sea of Galilee like thousands of bags

of Doritos, flummoxed beachcombers gathering it up
like netted tilapia, wolfing down each fluorescent morsel

like His sermons, each crunchy bite intoning *take up the whole armor
of God*. As if scrawled on the Tomahawk missile sliding from its bed:

don't be afraid: believe. Our Lamb of God high-tailing it atop the rising
waters at the Sheepshead Bay Yacht Club, with alligators and Jello,

with 600 piglets, 3,032 busted flour sacks, 2,184 cases of Molson.
Rome fully fallen, and like a La-Z-Boy uplifted in a flashflood torrent,

the apostles rising, Christianity catching on like PBR and beer nuts,
like Pop Rocks, Jesus juicing the citrus, and out gushes, with the pith

and the pulp, *Thou shalt not covet* and *Keep the Sabbath*, rendering
fatback into kielbasa, easing up on The Golden Rule long enough

to collect the miraculously-multiplying-from-a few-hundreds-
to-billions of fluttering-down dollars, looking the other way

because they're doomed, and besides, he's busy resurrecting
the glugging molasses, the tumbling hams, healing the wounds

of all who took a turn too fast, gashed their heads as a sugar beet load
overtook a swath of Dallas. Sweet Jesus! We're all going down

like a flotilla of entrails and skimmings. The bees cannot save us,
the bunnies cannot save us, the Savior cannot save us. We must

make our way in our own sticky, sanguineous stream, our own
exploding sperm whale. Decline and fall, decline and fall,

toward the wrecking ball of eternal *who knows?*

FROM

GRAVITY ASSIST

(2019)

SONG OF WEIGHTS AND MEASUREMENTS

For there is a dram.
For there is a farthing.
A bushel for your thoughts.
A hand for your withered heights.

For I have jouled along attempting
to quire and wisp.

For I have sized up a mountain's meters,
come down jiffy by shake to the tune
of leagues and stones.

For once I was your peck-ish darling.

For once there was the measure
of what an ox could plow
in a single morning.

For once the fother, the reed, the palm.

For one megalithic year I fixed my gaze
on the smiling meniscus, against the gray wall
of graduated cylinder.

For once I measured ten out of ten
on the scale of pain.

For I knew that soon I'd kiss goodbye
the bovate, the hide and hundredweight.

For in each pinch of salt, a whisper of doubt,
for in each medieval moment, emotion,

like an unruly cough syrup bottle, uncapped.
For though I dutifully swallowed

my banana doses, ascended, from WELCOME
to lanthorn, three barleycorns at a time,
I could not topple the trudging, trenchant cart.

For now I am forty rods from your chain and bolt.
For now I am my six-sacked self.

INSTEAD OF A FATHER

a volcano. A girl puzzling through long division between eruptions. A girl working hard to discern the intervals between disturbances. It was a kind of having to duck from the pumice. It was like the chunk of anthracite in your third-grade classroom, the one the teacher couldn't stop talking about. It was like the chained dogs at Pompeii—it was that pitch, one of the many greatest hits of the 70s. Steadfast like breathing in the finest particles, the ones that lodge in your blood. Like a cubic mile of ash and mud and rock. A seismic jolt followed by an explosion. It was like a heat surge scorching every eukaryotic cell, its Golgi apparatus, its smooth endoplasmic reticulum and its rough endoplasmic reticulum, each *you kernel* singed.

•

REPORT YOUR UNUSUAL PHENOMENON

Seen it myself as a girl—fire the size of a jet plane.
Race to tell my mother, who tells me not to lie.

And why should a mother, why should anyone
these will-o'-the-wisps gone wild, this spun silk

spattering brilliant streams, this yellow washtub
bouncing down a boulevard, traveling a city block,

crashing into a barn, killing the horse inside?
Why this buttery *boules de feu*, this *kugelblitz*

riding the center lane, buzzing the Sunday ham,
these sparkly basketballs striking the Golden Temple,

carving trenches, bulldozing peat, busting down doors?
Came at me like a comet. Blew my shirt right off.

Sizzling and cracking like bacon frying,
like candle flames nothing less than three feet

from my nose. Several physicists, a loud crash,
my sanity, especially here in the Midwest.

Not some sort of wacko President
of Find the Children. A grandma of three!

Half the timeframe fuzzy, but it rotated
on the sill like two fists, coiled tinsel, traffic signal

blinking amber, a novelty glass ball. Fizzed
like one of those fizzer sticks. I knew no one'd

believe me, that feeling taking laundry
from the dryer, but they weren't chirping,

not at all in a Figure 8, so I hung up quickly.
Just a blue mist, loose screw, ringing phone.

A hammer made of tinfoil, a hula-hoop of light.
Just me and my dear daddy (daddy saw it too).

Just leaving the house the same way it arrived.

MY ENVIRONS

I say warbling vireo
and a turbo jet drops from my tongue.
I say trill while a mower groans away
the cottonwood breeze. A bird says *If I see you,
I'm gonna seize you and squeeze you till you squirt*
as a line of cars slashes its psalms like linticels
on bark. How best to solve this natural /
unnatural dichotomy if not by clapping one
or both hands? *Scritch,* says the squirrel,
x, x, x, say those who solve for *y,* bye-bye
says the glacial moraine. I am multiplying
existence times the peculiar tufts of dozing
owls. Mice make their own sound. Who
can say who's more astonished? A person
mishears *momentous* as *moment,* falls into
a verdant complacency, sleepy as a dog
on a rug where nothing/everything's in flux.

GERBILS IN SPACE

And geckos. Fruit flies, kernels of corn.
Amoebas and bacteria. Black mice

and white mice. Once upon a time a dog
named Laika ascended in Sputnik 2,

egregious PR on account of no plan
for a safe return. But once they figured out

re-entry, up went Belka and Strelka,
public support. Two Russian tortoises,

a posse of mealworms, a few dozen
wine flies, all aboard Zond 5, first

orbiting of the moon. Before a human
could venture into weightlessness,

six rhesus monkeys named Albert preceded,
each one charmed with his own uniquely

abysmal end—explosions, suffocation,
failing parachutes. The French launched

Felicette, electrodes jammed beneath
feline skin, transmitting her condition

to the safely on the ground. More than hers
a hundred miles above our penny-loafered feet,

I wonder about the condition of the brains
beneath our bouffanted, mop-topped heads,

of a wavering between staunchest enemies
and let's-do-this-moon-thing-together friends.

A dozen gerbils 350 miles above me as I type,
high-tech gadgets sucking up ethereal waste

for the broken-free and the gravity-blessed—
for the constantly pulled in, the constantly falling back.

ODE TO AUTOCORRECT

Because it changes O'Hare to o hate,
o hate, o hate—over and over, no matter
how many times I retype it. O hate, like

an American tune, an American fable
where, yo, you can enter an o hate
bathroom, take a selfie in the mirror

cuz your sister wants to see the pockets
of your Great American Rhinestone Jeans.
Because, on a street called Viewpoint,

I get home becomes *I get guns*, off a road
on a mission to kill every squirrel-ish
pedestrian. Because he was packing,

concealed, threatening to use it, use
his hands or feet. *My feet*, iamb
of a son of a birch, of a brick chatting

with the devil, with God, with a listener
not listening. Because he'd gone bonnets,
his garden bounty a faded wine, his wife's

linguine longing for a golden ear,
so I took her to the botanical gardens
in my getaway car, to a fruit on a vine,

but the limes went lemur, the night to nonfat,
the clear to catastrophic. Because driving away
from the *frog man* croaking hypocrite,

heavenly went down like a melting hedge,
a gal gone hog-tied, a fish crying, a tiger-
tiger togetherness, flight or fucked,

a heart, stroked, racing to its vicarious
carousel, a fungus lashed to a beam gone
beleaguered. Because he will kill her,

that's his plan: to kill us all. Can't commit
or commute, can't debone his breath,
can't take his acute paranoia, chalk it up

to cute. Because this here's a Josie
madhouse, a bedroom bedrock-locked.
Because *Blvd* morphed to *Bled*, spirit

summoned with a Ouija board. Because
soap holder went *love hen*, though love
had flown the Calycanthus

like the grilled portabellos messing
with his vowels. Please *please*, I pleaded
to the pleading day. Because prayer

is like a bread line, a penny for your
exploded mind. Because *lots of logs
to you*, ma, because *so sorry* went *poem*.

NEARLY EVERY SONGBIRD ON EARTH IS EATING PLASTIC

nearly every rip is a crisp pact,
nearly every step is a disabled piss,
a slip, a *psst*, is past, is past

the squawking headline, below
the photo of a juvenile herring gull
clasping in its beak, sailing in its scat,

ridding from its ass, the remains
of a Yoplait parfait. In 1960, 5%
of sea-faring avians ate plastic.

In 1960, fewer sporks, fewer caps,
fewer cigarette tips. By 1980,
the number had jumped to 80%,

a stirrer, straw, & Starbucks lid
explosion. Global production
doubles by the decade, global lips

part, global rods cast, global
disablers dig, global dips subtract.
By 2028, more plastic swirling

in that gargantuan garbage gyre,
that loosely collected rubbish
spectacle than all the plastic

factory-spat since plastic-ing began.
When auklets stab at shrink wrap,
when pigeon guillemots gulp

Doritos bags, there's no room
in a gut for a mollusk, a morsel
of crab. Punches holes

in their organs. Strips parts. Scraps
scripts. When birds chew Blowpop
wrappers, guzzle Glad bags,

courtship desists. When one bird
eats 200 pieces. When one bird,
piling and bridling, is trapped.

When one bird's track
departs. "If you add plastic
to a gut, it will make a difference,"

said the gadfly petrel never. Subtract
how many there were, take two away
from three. Take away: a voice

vamoosing, an attic collapsing,
a number deeply dinged, teetering
on cast away, on doused, on dropping to nil.

STILL LIFE WITH MOTORCYCLE REVVING, WAILING SIREN, AMERICAN GOLDFINCH TRILL

Still life with cell phone, sorrel, beeping alarm.

    Still life with hovering flies, jet heading south toward SeaTac, 6:25.

Still life with crying toddler, catkins, arugula badly needing thinning.

    With gnat swarm, half empty glass of wine, one struggling ant

floating atop. Still life that will never be a still life, will never be,

    still I imagine what Dali, with his flare for the grandiose,

with his love of everything Velazquez, would make of this most vernal

    of vernal equinox. If I were Dalí (*jee jee jee jee jee*) the grass

would morph to a carpet of toothy smiles. As Dali, the kale sprouts

    mustachioed. But no, no, too easy—Dali cannot be reduced

to floating lips, a flourish of facial adornment. Yet, if Dali got his hands

    on this yard, on this psyche, he'd anoint them *Garden Caused*

by the Flight of a Gilded Flicker Around an Andalusian Dog a Second

    Before the Next Siren; *Past-due Blossoms with Devotion*

and Longing; *Poplar of the Inscrutable Conundrum*; *The Yellow Cedar*

    of Ponderous Faucet. All the while the robin cheery-upping its ass off.

Dali sailing off on a landlocked paddleboard, where Dali, I'm sure, embracing

    the local beach scene in a town where the green stuff's legal.

Oh, Dali.

    Sometimes you disturb me. When I pilgrimaged to St. Petersburg

for a glimpse of your soupy violins, your lynched eggs, your hallucinating

    toreador, *je me sentai pleine*, though a little unnerved. Always,

you were strange like Venus decked out in drawers, in pom-pom pasties,

    like a white lobster replacing a telephone's receiver, initially

jarring, though really what better ear-piece to commune with the populace?

    A faculty for Lorca-inspired tour de force is why I bequeath you

a yellow-rumped warbler's *chug-a-chugga-chug* of admiration.

    Witnessing your waxed mustache tango, I'm a little

immortal—*un peu artistique*—like I could—when the sirens cease,

    when the engines, when the cranky child melts

like a goopy blue clock, possess your fluent grace, a vibrant spurge—

    alive and lime-y, drunk with persistent excess.

BUMBLEBEES ARE MADE OF ASH

The day is a dragonfly hovering in the Timothy. It could rain for months
before the sun goes down. An orange buoy bobs while a sparrow
sings through a wall. The world smells of cedar, skunk spray,
a sedge's sharp edge. The cat's ears clear their throats,
prepare to speak. Kinnell called it "the inexhaustible
freshness of the sea." As if you could imitate
a preening cormorant. As if she'd said *can't
learn this way*, but you heard *can't live*,
destiny's dangling web. A horse
82 miles from its barn while
your brain swings open
like a giant pink
gate.

SPACE PROBE PANTOUM

Voyager 1 is leaving home.
Solar winds have slackened.
We didn't know; we didn't know
there'd be a transition zone.

Solar winds have slackened.
Particles from here and there: hello!
Who knew there'd be a transition zone
at the edge of a windless edge.

Particles from here and there: hello!
When the poles switch we'll be certain.
At the edge of a windless edge,
in a zone we've never known.

When the poles switch we'll be certain.
Unexpected, this zipping and zooming
in a zone we've never known.
We call this part the bow shock.

Unexpected, this zipping and zooming.
We're safe here with our sun.
We call this part the bow shock.
The exit, they say, will be rough.

We're safe here with our sun.
Not like a footprint on the moon.
The exit will be rough,
won't be all at once,

not like a footprint on the moon.
Like some strange angel
it won't be all at once.
Flitting around on the fringe

like some strange angel,
we know we're nearly there,
flitting around on the fringe.
Us stuff nearly gone,

we know we're nearly there.
Voyager 1 is leaving home,
us stuff nearly gone:
we didn't know; we didn't know.

PEACH GLOSA

Ah! And red; and they have peach fuzz, ah!
They are full of juice and the skin is soft.
They are full of the color of my village
And of fair weather, summer dew, peace.

~ Wallace Stevens, "A Dish of Peaches in Russia"

Slid out of me like stones,
like peonies and roses,
pricked like a holly bush,
lulled me with the hymns of weevils.
Loud like the lion that can kill,
flew out of me like cheetahs,
took hold of me like lice, like love.
Ripped me open like a cougar.
Rose up at me like a cream-bellied cobra.
Ah! and red; and they have peach fuzz, ah!

Clattering and weeping. Diapering
and digging. Exuberant singing,
firecats leaping. Peaches, more
peaches! Crates of velvety freestones.
In a basket, at breakfast, with a wasp.
Hail, pale stranger, come down
from the Kunlun Shan Mountains.
Beware of leaf curl, brown rot, beware
the speckled emperor, the catapult moth.
They are full of juice and the skin is soft.

Bloodmeal, bonemeal, or stunted growth.
Peach wood arrows to shoot away evil;
peach wood wands to ward away the bad.
Caravaggio's memorable discolorations,
molted and wormholed, Monet and Rubens
speaking the truth, through peach and leafage,
from their hearts and tongues. Budded or grafted
from a suitable rootstock. Budded or grafted,
my dear luscious darlings, my dappled courage.
They are full of the color of my village.

They grow like stars. They grow like mountains,
like fissures, an inch or six a year. Measure
themselves against a lazy yellow wall. Compete
to see who'll ripen first. Stevens said,
of parenting, it's a "terrible blow to poor
literature," Holly, peach of his reason,
pen stilled till she reached the age of nine,
firecat closing his big, bright eyes.
They are not ours, not ours to keep, spice
of fair weather, summer dew, peace.

BREAK-AWAY EFFECT

In a study published in the April 1957 issue of Aviation Medicine, *35 percent of training astronauts and cosmonauts reported having experienced a strange feeling of having broken the bonds of the terrestrial sphere. Psychologists referred to this phenomenon as the break-away effect.*

~ Mary Roach, *Packing for Mars*

As if my body were a door or gate, cabinet
bereft of its rational rations, they worried

I'd unhinge, become the lunatic saboteur.
They barred my hands from touching

their switches and dials, my access
to the manual. And here I am—

surprise!—your peaceful giant,
benevolent king of the cosmos;

it's all I can do to keep from belting out
The Motherland hears, the Motherland knows /

where her son flies in the sky. Down there,
every sunset's a smashed egg; up here,

dusk's a pink-cheeked *devochka*, a violet
violence, orange of longing stilled. They said

I'd panic, shock of fathomless vacuum akin
to slicing a kayak through the Bering Strait,

never having commandeered a pair of paddles
freed from their clips. Instead, I'm glued

to the porthole, to the wispy beards of mountains,
stray-hair rivers, lemony fields of wheat, light

as if streaming from the stained glass of Pokrovsky
Cathedral. Each dawn a powder-blue halo,

and me with just one wish: to never return.

FROM

THIS ONE WE CALL OURS

(2024)

WHAT THEY SAID

That they'd studied four percent of the sky.
That there's this thing called the ionosphere.
That it's like looking at the sky

from the bottom of a swimming pool.
That they were counting black holes
with instruments 10x better than before,

plus algorithms, plus all these words
I didn't understand, but four percent
of the sky, but in that narrow band

to the north they found 25,000,
which means in the remaining 96%
there could be close to half a million

more. And that's what they plan to do:
count every black hole in the sky. Count
every event horizon, every instance

of swirling infinite blackness,
of the place of no return,
of the sucking power no Dyson

has ever known. The place of spaghetti-
fication. The *who knew there were so many*,
the *who knew they were visible to us*,

not just one but 25,000, each in a galaxy
like our own—substantial, giant-armed,
borne of what spilled from Hera's breast

when she realized she was nursing another
woman's child, the baby Hercules.
With its 100 thousand million stars,

with its 100 billion planets, with its one
planet with one ocean. This one we
float on, this one we call ours.

ONCE,

before this lake turned the color of ripened cherries, before
there was a word for *weapon* or *distance* or *phone*,
a star finished up its nucleosynthesis,

exploded its hydrogen, helium, neon and nitrogen, its sulfur
and iron, all over cosmos town. No one was around,
no one with vision or a craving for lemons.

All there was: stars and exploding stars seeding the universe
with magnesium and carbon, with graphite and diamonds.
All this, and what all else, collected into a pomegranitic

bulge that became our sun, that became the rocky planets
and the gaseous ones, that became the generous
light through pines, us and our armpit glands,

us and our *Mother, may I? No, you may not.* This was how it began,
before it cooled enough for worms and flukes, way cooler
than that instant when everything that would ever be

became, though it would be a while before figs and plumage,
rain drops and touch. But soon we had gnawing,
and soon we had fathers. Falling water

and falling in love. Before long there was work, and there was wine.
Observances like the Feast of Assumption. Soon after
there was rot and grief. But before that: electrons

and quarks. Protons and neutrons. Somehow, we got hummingbirds
and pavement, dorsal fins and cilantro. Somehow, anger
and shame and faith. Now we are a place

for lace and egrets. Now we have mouthwash and redwoods.
It's sweet like a good pear, sour like probiotic yogurt.
It began and it seems, like a novel

by Tolstoy, like it will never end, but one day—zip-zap, zap-zip—
the sun will supernova, and we will give back
our copper and plutonium, our aluminum

and titanium. The calcium in our bones will contract into dimensionless
singularity, along with all our shiny silver fillings, our stalks
of wheat, our shocks of turquoise hair.

TWO HUNDRED MILLION YEARS AGO THIS WAS ALL A SEA FLOOR,

says the vineyard owner in the Dundee Hills. He says he switched
from tequila to wine because each time his father borrowed
his Ford Bronco, he paid him back with Riesling.

The Natasha block is named for his oldest daughter. There you'll find
the Pinot reserve. Aspen rules the cuvée, Jordan the Chardonnay.
He moved up from San Bernadino for the cooler summers,

the coastal mountains, but now he says they need to irrigate, now the summers
stretch out and out in a series of 116-degree days.
We come bearing not so much a thirst

as a need for a buzz, for stories about the knock-kneed vines
planted thirty years ago, when we were knocking knees
in a booth at a pub where we first met.

The owner shuffles toward a couple sipping the Old Block Pommard,
its garnet charm, his hands trembling like his grape leaves
in the early afternoon breeze.

Last week we were in our twenties, wandering a forest, learning to distinguish
pentstemon from lupine, digging out a knife from a daypack to harvest
Chicken of the Woods from the trunk of a western hemlock.

The soils of sandstone, loess, and loam make for a flinty forward,
say the tasting notes. Sandstone from the ocean, loess
from the glaciers, loam from the thirty-six times

this valley flooded when a melting glacier unblocked a massive lake.
Spans of time difficult for a human brain as we wander down
the rows of new plantings, black hoses, parched dirt.

DURING THE CRETACEOUS OUR COUNTRY WAS DIVIDED FOR SIXTY MILLION YEARS

by an inland sea. The fissure was 2,000 miles long, 600 feet wide,
and 2,500 feet deep. On the left side, Laramidia.
On the right, Appalachia. Back then,

the landscape was recognizable to both sides. To both,
clams were the size of small area rugs,
turtles as big as Dodge Darts.

Both agreed *Elasmosaurus* had a streamlined body,
paddle-like limbs, a 23-foot-long neck.
If a Ginsu shark swam past,

both would laugh about how it got its name: its ability to slice
and dice. No one argued whether *Hesperornis,* a cormorant-
like bird chowed down whole by mosasaurs,

was flightless or not, whether it used its bill and teeth
to hunt down bony fish. Maybe because unity
depends on a baseline of shared reality,

all agreeing shark teeth are shark teeth, crinoid lilies
are crinoid lilies, that a fish's jaw cannot be fungible,
that you can't swap out a toothed tongue

for a smooth one. On both sides of the divide, dinosaurs roamed.
On both sides earth was earth, the landscape recognizable
to the creatures on either side.

No one on the left side and no one on the right side
rubbed their eyes and said Nope, nope,
no such thing as a plesiosaur,

no such thing as a coccolithophore. The schism was literal,
not figurative. Caused by subduction, one plate colliding
into another. At the end of the Cretaceous,

the sea dried up. Now the sea is all the middle states, those who voted
red and those who voted blue. Where the sea was: the chalky
remnants of a sea, of bivalves, their shiny pearls.

NO RAIN

It's October and it hasn't rained.
Why are we surprised?
Why did we think

it couldn't happen here, our home,
the Pacific Northwest? Moss,
mushrooms, mist.

The lake so low, puzzled geese.
Who wants to think about it?
It's October

and it hasn't rained. I check my phone:
Seattle 71 / Smoke. I meet a friend
who asks me to write a secret

on a scrap of paper. He does the same,
then takes out his lighter, burns
what we wrote, embers

floating above the lake, adding our smoke
to an AQI in the red, a 13,000-acre fire
seventy miles away.

The seven-day forecast: *sun, sun, part sun, part sun,
sun, sun, sun.* I don't want to ask
but I know.

The geese honk, fly south, but it's not fall
without the rain. The lake so low,
exposing a sunken forest.

It's October, time to plant spinach and kale.
We fill the watering can, dream
of picking chanterelles.

WHEN WE SAY IT'S THE LITTLE THINGS

we really do mean it, a friend announcing, at the end
of a long phone call, in which she shares her love
of *The Red Shoes* and *Moulin Rouge,*
 "I love you,"

how good that feels when you wake in the middle of the night,
the worth of that unexpected gesture like a lover
who cleans out the dishwasher filter without
being asked. It's the taste of that first sip

of coffee, rich and strong, the *Mr. Coffee* cup warmer
on your desk. It's having the right pen; it's a full
water bottle, a piece of orange-cranberry bread,
warm and moist, crunchy with walnuts.

We also love the big things, like Fatu and Najin, the last
two white rhinos, a mother and her daughter.
You can watch them on *YouTube,*
snorfling in the Kenyan dust,

the calming hum of insects all around them, which is more
of the little things, because mostly it's those, the insects
outweighing our human bulk seventeen times,
bush crickets and pill bugs, bot flies

and army ants that, when the time comes,
will make quick work of our little
and big bodies, our veined
and ventricled hearts.

OH, AUTOLYSIS

All it means is self-digestion, our body's microbes doing the work
of undoing. All it means is the miracle of what had sustained us
morphing into what's needed to reduce us to nitrogen

and phosphorous, to return us to the Earth where we'll make a rich soil
for basil and thyme. The book says *leak* as cells break down,
says *rigor mortis*, says in each gut dwell

hundreds or thousands of species, which after death become
a thanatomicrobiome, from *Thanatos,* god of death,
brother of Hypnos, kin to Oizys, god of suffering,

and Moros, god of doom, the holy book of woe, the opposite
of a heart-shaped box of chocolates, the microbes,
like a rowdy mob, making their way

to the liver, the heart and brain, then everything in between.
The most hallowed parts of the body now a credenza
on which to put their feet up,

rifle through the desks of the spleen, the half-finished crossword puzzles
of the lymph nodes. I wondered how it happens, the why
of exploding abdomens, and here it is:

our bodies pre-equipped with the critters who break us down
from long-legged Vegas dancers to fodder for a cluster
of mushrooms. *Molecular death,*

the book called it. Full on slippage into the soil.
And what do we carry? What have we carried?
Eyes that had noted the mouthlike petals

of snapdragons, the sticky white pods of milkweed,
hands that had gathered them into bouquets.
Hands that had held.

LETTER TO A POST-APOCALYPTIC COCKROACH

with apologies to Matthew Olzmann

You probably think we hated frost, rime, grout, hail, icy rivers,
icy glaciers, icy shelves keeping icy glaciers
from plunging into the sea. Probably,

you think we hated gorillas, orangutans, Edith's checkerspot, the nine-spotted lady beetle
as much as we loved Toyota Tundras, Styrofoam coolers, Starbucks lids,
the fluorocarbons in our extra-hold Aqua-Net.

Knowing every minute what we were doing, metric ton by metric ton,
I bet you think we were incapable of dancing wildly in the aisles
at a what's-left-of-the-Dead show, but you'd be wrong.

Back then, when we still had the Amur leopard, a whopping total of eighty-four
because poachers killed them for their bones, steeped them in rice wine,
sold it as medicine. When we still had

Western red cedars, sword fern, Oregon grape, salal, twinflower, inside-out flower,
queen's cup, red huckleberry, and the one-sided pyrola. Man, did we ever admire
the 44,000-mile migration route of the Arctic Tern. Hard to believe,

but there were seasons. Skiing. Low-lying vacation homes. Cities named Manhattan,
New Orleans, Miami. Grass died in the summer, turned emerald in September.
Do I have to tell you it wasn't all panic or worry? That some, in protest,

threw soup at famous art, but pretty much the days went on as they always had
while headlines shared the Antarctic was warming five times faster
than the global average? What were we doing,

I guess you want to know. Combusting our engines. Turning up the thermostat.
Paying eight cents, at the checkout line, for a paper bag. Buying stuff,
then donating it to the Global South, or tossing it into methane-

seething landfills. The ocean warmed 1.5 degrees, which to many seemed piddly
(most didn't know water expands as it warms). Polar ice sheets thinned.
Gail-force winds caused concrete piers to pound into each other,

break apart. Rivers fell from the sky while we fought hard for our freedom
to eat beef burgers whenever we liked. And then the humans were gone,
and the Earth continued to spin.

POEM WRITTEN ONE HUNDRED YARDS FROM MY MOTHER'S GRAVE

Of course, the sky is cloudless. Of course, when the sun sets,
we can see Gemini, four planets in a row,
Taurus's bright eye.

I'm standing on the top deck of her brother's cabin,
the one forged from cedar logs, the cabin
she never got to see,

never got to wrap herself in my Aunt Judy's red, white, and blue-checked throw,
add a log to the fire, joke about the icy outhouse toilet seat,
sing along to a battery-powered radio's

"Baby, It's Cold Outside." She's down past a grove of oaks,
or her bones anyway, in the most peaceful spot
on this 160-acre homestead.

Sitting beside her marking stone, a V-shaped cluster of Ozark sandstone,
limestone, and chert, I knew she couldn't be gone, couldn't be
in some kind of pearly-gated heaven.

Of course, when a pileated woodpecker flies close, lets go
a high-pitched *e-e-e-e-e-e-e-e-e*, I know it's her
as well as I know it's not,

but that something was making sure, when the universe formed, gravity
wasn't too strong—not enough to break atoms apart, not so weak
they couldn't hold them together, expanding into now.

SELF-PORTRAIT AS SOUTHERN RESIDENT ORCA

For everybody *I'm speechless! Damn it, I gotta go get my camera!*
For *this must be the happiest pod.*
For you can hear them saying *there she goes again. Big one! Wow!*
For you can hear them clapping, laughing.
For I swim through the research proving there is no difference in the lifespan
of being born at Sea World or in the wild.
For 700,000 years of genetic distinction, 700,000 years of a distinct dialect evolving.
For I was misnamed *whale killer* by Spanish explorers.
For I am a dolphin.
For each year I ingest the seven million quarts of motor oil washing into the Salish Sea.
For despite being banned in 1979, each day I push through 1.5 billion pounds of PCBs.
For in my fat stores I carry your coal mining, electric appliance dependence, insecticides.
For because of you I brush against carcinogenic furans.
For I am a mother carrying her dead newborn. For I have been carrying him for days.
For thanks to my contaminated milk, he is even more toxic than I.
For you might call this behavior a tour of grief, but I have been driving my baby
to the surface so he can take a breath.
For my solitude grows scarce.
For your ships interfere with my clicks, whistles, and pulses, with knowing
where the salmon are—species, speed, size.
For the sea and I are both wide.
For the water I glide through is poisoned with viscosity index improvers; for the
lapping is laced with alkaline additives and sealants; for if you read more closely,
search more carefully,
you will learn PCBs were not banned but permitted in smaller concentrations.
For I can certainly experience intense emotion.
For Monsanto's CEO makes 19 million a year but the Chemical Action Plan
lacks funding; for there is no government strong enough to save me.
For behold my spy-hopping!

For who can resist my one-syllabled, Darth Vader-like exhale?
For Google *biomagnification*.
For the dusty road is my demise.
For the highway's yellow line, I die.
For I'm corralled not by my mistakes but yours.
For the doors of my duration are closing.

TIME AND DISTANCE

Time is like a sandal in a cave: here I was.
If no heat is exchanged, time does not exist.
The little blue macaw is gone. The distance grows.

What one needs is a helping verb, a word like *does*.
What one gets instead is a cosmic abyss.
Time is like a sandal in a cave: here I was.

There are planets no telescope will disclose.
Though no one's sure, our nature is to shift.
The little blue macaw is gone. The distance grows.

There should be more silence, less applause.
We should be more like Neptune grass. It persists.
Time is like a sandal in a cave: here I was.

Horseshoe crabs preceded the dinosaurs.
Each spring they convene for a spawning blitz.
The little blue macaw is gone. The distance grows.

If you come bearing peanuts or a cage, a crow recalls.
For just one day, let me grow a carapace.
Time is like a sandal in a cave: here I was.
The little blue macaw is gone. The distance grows.

FAILED ATTEMPT AT MYTHMAKING

I wanted to write about terns. Which terns? The Caspians nesting
on a very hot roof. What the conservation scientist said:
They confuse the dust from the cement plant

with beach. During the heatwave the flightless chicks
jumped. Jumped. Fell into gutters, got stuck.
Some made it to the ground,

where they also got stuck. I asked a friend how to write a poem
about animals in pain. *What if you wrote it
as a short poem? Seven lines max.*

I'd been reading Sappho, had brief on the brain,
but this wasn't a fragmented lyric situation.
The newspaper said *A number*

were too injured and euthanized. A number,
but no number provided. The dead birds
were juveniles. The friend said

*Maybe you could write it as an Ars poetica,
or just keep writing past the end.*
The ones that lived

were treated for burns on their feet. And fluid support,
which I guess means water. A number,
however, were not.

A volunteer with Audubon said he'd never seen
birds jump from their nests from such a height,
but it had never been 106 in Seattle.

I could bring in Hephaestus, god of fire,
patron saint of craftsmen.
His workshop's inside

a volcano. I could bring in Dante's *Inferno: Welcome to the city
of woe. Welcome to everlasting sadness ... to the grave cave.
You, who have no hope ...* etc.

My friend wrote: *I think it has to do with imagining things
have agency beyond our knowledge, which they do.*
They mistake our cement piles for beach,

a tar-covered roof for a prime nesting site.
I could mention the patron saint
of animals, I could write past,

so far past—when they're not,
when we're not—
but I won't.

SOUL RECKONING

I'm skimming through a book called *Spook:
Science Tackles the Afterlife.*
It turns out gravity

doesn't hold for souls; they drift, like loons
between dives, into eternity, along
with NASA's detritus—urine bags,

miles of copper wire, a chunk of Apollo 12. Knowing this,
I leave behind five decades' worth of fear
that I'll die and no longer *be*,

that consciousness must be contained in a body.
To get here, I said goodbye to guilt, to regret
I missed the funeral,

to wishing I was there when my second cousin Timmy
found the lost key to Uncle John's truck,
then sped off to lower her casket

into a hole, to chime or chip in about the words to engrave
on her marking stone. On all of this I punted,
from all of this I'd excused myself

on account of a plane ride, the specter of unmasked sobbing,
singing, cookies and punch. To get here, I took a road
rutted with limestone creatures

laid down in a shallow sea. My travel speed is two inches per year,
same as the moon from Earth. A little less bound by gravity.
A little more free.

THAT SUMMER

we didn't have enough tomatoes for caprese.
Our sun-gold summer a bust. A friend said
your plants are dying; he was right.

The leaves like maps chewed by moths.
We resigned ourselves to heirlooms
from the store. Delicious, I said,

almost as good, almost a summer but also not—
the floating docks never pulled by a tug
to their beaches, the diving boards

in storage, as if all summer it was winter, a strange season
of heat-struck hydrangeas, an abundance of hunger
for touch, of opening doors, inviting in

the kinglets and wrens. Autumn: here it comes, here it opens
into falling, into steely blankets, into greening grass
where summer had been a *Keep Moving* sign,

a warning: *Crowded Parks Lead to Closed Parks*.
Not a single tomato to can. Something
went wrong in the garden.

Now, the maples are catching fire. Frost overtakes the mud.
I put away my flower-print skirts, turn my attention
to the flames.

EVERYTHING ENDS

but so what. In the sultry nights of August, I'll unravel –
wanna join me? We can pant ourselves pantless,

share a double brushfire on the raucous. Together
we can close the book on the Uncertainty Principle,

load up, unwaning, at Wingstop, discuss the sorrow
of burned beaks. Free the crows, you say, and I raise

a toast to a small, uninhabited island, a boisterous whale,
a purity stone, a planet without smoke. Because pleasure

counts big time. Because days spent in a tender mess
are unrecoverable. Naked and floodlit, cocooned

in the opposite of random, we remind ourselves
of the importance of seaweed and seasons,

of each and every bacteria, how we're more
microbe than human. If everything ends,

why are you sharpening your sorrow,
running to catch the discomfort.

FROM

TERMINAL SURREAL

(2025)

FLYING RATS

with apologies to Mary Oliver

Actually? You do have to be good.
For real? You kinda do have to walk,
if not literally on your knees,
then figuratively on your knees,
or if not on your "knees," then
in really cruddy, falling apart
grandma tennies with worn-out
orthotics she bought back in the '90s
at Kmart. For, like, a hundred miles—
from downtown Los Angeles
to the Bakersfield McDonald's.
Also, guess what? You do have to say
I'm sorry many times a day for things
like forgetting to tighten the faucet,
or leaving the gas on, or hitting
your kids, even if only once
on the bottom. Not gonna lie:
you can't go around all jellyfish,
all shell-less mollusk, scrolling
Instagram or watching *Love Island*.
We can talk to each other about
what pains us (me: not going to visit
my deathbed mother; you: having
to gain weight), but let's be honest:
saying "Meanwhile the world goes on"
doesn't cut it. Why? Because yeah,
there's sun and pebbles, prairies
and trees, mountains and rivers,

but let's not airbrush out the number
of acres of US forest lost to wildfires
this past summer: seven and a half
million. Meanwhile the geese
are shitting all over the playground grass,
the walkways and cement barriers.
Not high up, but dragging their butts
across mowed-down blackberry brambles.
Okay, so you're lonely, and the world
offers you *Itself?* Calls to you like
one of these cobra chickens? Yeah,
yeah, pretty harsh. Pretty f-ing harsh.

WHAT'S TERRIBLE

~ *after Dorianne Laux*

When the alpenglow fades and the ridicule flares. When the morass appears, three-quarters pestilence, one-quarter shale. A whining moth that morphs to a motif. A manager defending a pervert. A mandate to spray Roundup. A flea soiree. Flawed soil. When the moor is too briquette to sleep. When the stripes are too broad to see the rorqual for the *Cyamus*. A broken fin. Downturn far enough to throb. Jettison when it loses its riffle. Nonsense you can't plait. A ridiculing jester, harder to listen to than traitors, than sitars at a Lunatic Éclair Siege. When the ATM eats your cardigan, your caress. You forgot to charge your phone. The plantains didn't align. You need chemo, but CVS is flush out of toxins. Wastelands. Horsewhips. No map, no toilet paper, no headlamp. The sound of windbags through pineapple groves. The scent of Vieux-Boulogne. The menacing shadows of hemlocks.

POSSIBLE DIAGNOSIS

What's that stone, that one stone edging
toward the edge? In Italian, for spider,
say *ragno*. Say *web*

in a musical spell. I was with a friend,
on my last round. When I told her
I might be dying,

she was my dictator of snow, holding me
and my gone-berserk nerves.
I told her my mother

puts the relevant clues in crossword puzzles:
Riley, *refs*, and *palomas*. Isn't she
the best cheerer-upper ever?

Maybe I'm a witch for the drama cauldron,
maybe I just need more sleep, more
nooky, cookies-n-cream.

Old and unheavy, in need of rest. God?
I don't quite believe, but at night
I let myself go fetal,

hands pressed like that plastic pair Svennie found
at a thrift store in Shelton. To breathe.
To swallow. Now I understand:

incurable might not be the worst thing. Upsides, like creasing
the cloth napkins, carrying them down to their home
in a living room drawer,

admiring the spotted towhee making a ruckus in dead leaves.
I thought it would be like a thumb coming down
on a spider's body, but it was not.

ORDERS OF OPERATION

First thing, my hair began to weep. Wept like sea oats, the roots of which
are forty feet deep. First thing, my torso quivered like mud
in a 192-mile-an-hour wind. Like a seed head

in a Category 6, its vibrating underground rhizomes. One night,
in my bathroom mirror, I thought I saw my heartbeat
in my bicep. What was that quote

about a bitter heart? *In the desert I saw a creature, naked, bestial* . . .
A naked, bestial creature eating his bitter heart. What a wild image,
right? Liking the bitter taste *Because it is bitter,* the way an osprey

must love the taste of salt on its mouth as it dives for a fish,
succeeds. It must know that feeling of victory, of settling
into a palmetto, or perching at the top of a building

to feast. After a while, I listened with my eyebrows. After a while,
I listened to the sunlight in my pectorals and glutes,
the non-noise of sleep, which made me anxious.

And ahhh, what was this thing with my voice, why was it getting harder
to swallow and speak? When I googled, I found hideous things.
To lightly fly away, like a rosy maple moth. Slowly,

but not too slow. To flutter in the key of yellow and pink,
without coughing or wheezing,
without a bat-like resistance.

To go without weeping or creaking, without too much hoopla,
like these little precious creamy-white wings,
like these rosy-pink markings

on the margins and bases, which do a kind of breezy,
like oat grass, which does a little able flying,
then slows down so lightly, so lovely.

SINCE YOU'RE ALIVE

you bother less with things like pants,
stroll into the kitchen at 5 a.m.
wearing the $5 briefs you found in a pile

of $5 briefs at Target, floppy pink flowers
against a green background, note just how bony
your bony ass, as this thing called *denervation*

begins its dance in your biceps and shoulders,
though isn't it more like August in the vineyards
of the Willamette Valley? Crushing time.

Nothing's bleeding, no ghosts signaling
you're gonna be fine, but when you call your brother,
tell him you want some of who you were

in the family plot, a light goes on
in your beat-up Elantra:
What's that goddamn light doing on?

Though the sky's unlit by 4 p.m., unlit for over fifteen hours,
which was always rough, but now, my God.
At home, you focus on the fireplace

while fearing the same flutter beneath your right eye,
which your love insists is barely visible,
but for how long? And what had I

wished for? Had it been Venice,
the Uffizi, one more hike to Mason Lake,
Spiraea douglasii along its shore?

All of it, of course, all of it in unison,
that scent of early decay, that first
turn from summer to fall.

WHEN I LEARN CATASTROPHICALLY

is an anagram of *amyotrophic lateral sclerosis*.
When I learn I probably have a couple years,
maybe (catastrophically) less, crossword puzzles
begin to feel meaningless, though not the pair
of buffleheads, not the red cardinal of my heart.
The sky does all sorts of marvelously uncatastrophic
things that winter I shimmy between science
& song, between widgeons & windows, weather
& its invitation to walk. Walking, which becomes
my *lose less*, my *less morsels*, my *lose smile*
while *more sore looms*. Sometimes I wander
for hours, my mile pace over half an hour,
everyone passing the lady at dusk talking
to herself about *looming rooms, soil lies, ire
& else*. Chuckling about my mileage gone down
the toilet, I plant the *rose* of before, the *oil* of after.
As each breath elevates to miracle, I become
both more & less of who I'd been, increasingly
less concerned about the dishes in the sink,
more worried about the words in my notebooks,
all those unfinished poems. I remember the fear
of getting lost if I left the main trail. I remember
molehills, actual molehills, piles of salty roe,
mountains of limes. Catastrophically, it's rare:
one in 500,000, but then I learned the odds
of being born: one in 42 billion, though not sure
how they calculate, or the chances of the cosmos
having just the right amount of force to not
break apart. *Less smiles. More lose. Miser miles.*
A sis & bro whom I'll leave like a sinking island,

Ferdinandea, that submerged volcano in Sicily,
though let's be real: I was more *pen mole* than *lava*,
more a looming annoyance than a bridge
to some continent. I'd wanted to be composted,
but it would cost 9K to convert me to dirt, so I opted
for whatever was easiest to carry across state lines,
some of me beside my mother & father, bits of me
on San Juan Island, at Jakle's Lagoon & Seward Park,
where I'd wandered like a *morose remorse*,
a *lore-less reel*, a *miser silo*, a doddering crow.

TO-DO LIST

of doom. To withdraw like a fly or amuse oneself
like a submarine in a fjord misnamed a canal.
To decide rain makes it worse,

but sun's bad too, but both are good.
When the answer to the question
is *die*.

When the father asks *when will we
tell the kids*, when die, when die,
when die.

Seeing the word *skull* reminds me of winter
in Santa Fe, O'Keeffe's obsession—
worn, bleached, jagged. Holy,

holey, and whole. Add: that it will never be
June in my spine. That the leaves
will return,

girls will converse, but the topaz truth went underground
with the scorpions my nephew knew where to find,
that I can't pant or paint or prance away

the traverse toward being a transient mom.
The salt of it, so not a honeycomb
of revive.

ABECEDARIAN WITH ALS

A little bit sane (a little bit not).
Blackbirds that turned out to be boat-tailed grackles.
Crows that cannot covert their fury of feathers.
Don't say Relyvrio reminds you of hemlock.
Every wave reassuringly governed by the moon, but what about riptides?
F*ck a duck!
Glad there's a joyful edge, though narrower than a willet's beak.
Hail in the forecast. A bitter taste:
it enables animals to avoid exposure to toxins.
Jaw stiffens, then relaxes. What will my body do next?
Kindness, we decide, is what we want to broadcast,
letting someone pull out in front of you in traffic,
make their turn, because the universe isn't elegant,
no one's really going anywhere important,
or running late to spin or vinyasa or
pilates. The neutral neutrons of the nucleus.
Quarks that are up, down, charm, strange, top, and bottom, though
rehab in the CD, a lunch date in Leschi, PT in Madrona—it happens.
Socrates died of centripetal paralysis, a prominent loss of sensation.
Terminal: I wish it was more like waiting out a storm with an $18.00 glass of pinot.
Unbound bound.
Very much looking forward to overcooked orzo and finely chopped squash.
What was that you assured me—when we die, we wake from a dream?
X marks the rear of the theatre—one shove of poison—into a pure realm.
You know we're all getting off at the same exit, right?
Zooey's wish: to pray without ceasing.

I DIDN'T UNDERSTAND KEATS'S "ODE TO A NIGHTINGALE"

until I was terminal, which when you think about it, how else are you supposed to understand lines like *My heart aches, and a drowsy numbness pains*, or *My sense, as though of hemlock I had drunk*? I mean, it was like the other day when I grabbed a pillow, placed it on the red Adirondack chair in our front yard, sat there listening to a song sparrow singing its ass off, along with a robin cheery-upping so damn much (beyond ironic). *Some dull opiate*, indeed! Ode, schmode, I was thinking, though I do love a praise song, am thankful and glad to proclaim that not only can I watch two eagles copulating in the tippy-top of a western red cedar, cry because they've found each other, are something like in love, and because earlier I saw them doing a locked-talons flip-glide over the lake, but I can get myself out of bed, wash my face, brush my teeth. No nightingales here in Seattle, but you get my approximate drift. *Sunburnt mirth!* I totally get it, as well as *a beaker full of the warm South*, which could be Death Valley, Cadiz, or fucking Matera! Some lady on YouTube said Keats is drunk at this point in the poem, but my take is he's contemplating suicide—a bubbly cocktail to snuff himself out because let's face it: being tubercular is worse than ALS: he shook and groaned with pain, whereas all I'm dealing with is *The weariness, a tad of fret*. My gray hairs aren't even shaking, but a friend I haven't spoken to in over forty years sent me a bouquet: pink roses and purple peas! I wonder, though, about those *viewless wings of Poesy*. Is that where we trot out this thing called negative capability? Did he want us to figure out why poesy is viewless, or did he want us to be uncertain? His brain is dull, as I'm sure mine will soon be, and shit, *here there is no light* is quite the heavy, but there are flowers on my table, and I remember Peggy, the red-haired girl who lived in Tofu House, raised by her grandparents cuz she was the eighth kid in an Irish brood—her parents done with raising kids. *Embalmed darkness*, which reminds me I need to figure out who's doing my cremation, or maybe pony up for Recompose. I'd prefer it if the days were shortening, if the plum tree across the street wasn't wildly bursting into bloom, but whaddya gonna do but listen to the siskins, flickers, and jays, watch them

hop from budded-to-budded branch? We've even got these from-who-knows-where
violets cropping up in our weedy beds, along with a *murmurous haunt of flies*,
so maybe I'll stick with cremation. Yeah, I think I finally get this poem—
I was never *half in love with easeful Death*—when I thought about *my quiet breath*,
when I thought *now more than ever seems it rich to die, / To cease upon the midnight
with no pain*, cuz who the fuck wants to be in pain? Yet if I knock myself off too soon,
my family won't get that big fat check, plus no more *dee-dee-dee* of chickadees.
Uncertainly, he calls *Adieu! adieu!* I guess the nightingale's petering out,
which is also Keats's *poesy*, no? Something's buried deep, though hopefully
the music never flees, the music that is poetry.

TERMINAL SURREAL

or is it surreal terminal? Something's going on
with my mitochondria. Something to do
with oxidation. My cells

need help with ridding my body of toxins, which explains
the bear bile I drank twice daily until it turned out
it was doing nothing

but making me nauseous. Surreal swirl of feta cheesecake
topped with macerated cherries. Ooh, that tastes good.
My husband calls to tell me he just heard

the first red-winged blackbird of the season, saw bald eagles
dive-bombing mergansers. I'm just sitting here pretending
I don't have ALS, that somehow, I'll live.

Fifty degrees and partly sunny: my kind of day! To forget,
while I'm listening to honking geese, that yesterday
a friend went into hospice,

that the amount of misery is equal to or greater than the number of eggs
a termite queen will lay in a lifetime—165 million.
I learned today about the mountain stone wētā,

a cricket that, when it gets cold, freezes 85% of its body. When the blizzard
passes, it comes back to life. Meanwhile, another eagle's flying overhead,
this one solo, heading south until it's out of sight.

SELF-ELEGIES

Because why not? Why not take the smashed pinecone
of my life, render it in purple? Why not dream of baking
thirteen pies, six bumbleberry, seven sour cherry? I wouldn't
press myself into a grief box, but I will confess I'm happiest
under a sleeping sky, love the darkness like I loved to run
through old-growth Doug firs and cedars. There's no more
rolled-out crust, no more loping strides or flour, but at midnight
I read a book about microbes and fungi, how these critters
find a way into us, never leave. It's the never-leaving part
I like. It's the memory of the Cuisinart loaded with dough,
the rolling out, crimping with a fork. No grief in the night,
though I'd welcome a northern shoveler, the green head
of a mallard. The Vaux's swifts that crowd the rising moon.
My husband's favorite tomato, the Jaune Flamme.

In a Plum Village meditation, a woman says *smile*,
so I smile, though sometimes I don't, though sometimes
I'm unable. Disabled is my smile, and a lot makes me cry.
I tell those who hear me sobbing I'm not sad, and it's true –
I'm moved when friends bring fennel soup or say I look,
well, undying, when I share my joy that my daughter
has said hello to my death, not exactly made friends
but isn't hysterical, and isn't that like a favorite song,
the unsilence of "The Sound of Silence"? She's smiling,
beautiful in her black cap-sleeve top and oversized jeans,
and so is everything out my bedroom window. I open
my curtains to the crows, to a scrub jay in the maple.
Accepting I'll do death alone like I've done most everything:
birth, growth, forgiveness, hunger, all these freaking feelings.

The other night I danced for the first time in months
to my favorite Sheryl Crow song – opens with guitar
and drums. She sings about catching a ride, how she
likes the brochure. I used to dance on my paddleboard
for hours. Ran down all sorts of winding roads,
getting closer. I could've never walked, but I walked
for sixty-two and a half years. Now I look out my window,
envy the dog walkers. Did I ever think I wouldn't be the one
jumping in? Each morning, I looked in the mirror,
said, "You're sure not your grandma!" Pridefully, smugly
able. When anything went. Now the green's mostly
what I see from my wheelchair. Getting into the *done,* I guess
you'd say. A little closer to no more Polish polkas,
no impromptu kitchen waltzing. To not feeling fine.

Maybe I was stained with mercury and malathion.
Maybe that time I ran through the fog of mosquito
repellent wasn't the best idea, though we all did it,
didn't we? When a friend told me to get a watch
to keep track of my miles, I didn't know it would
become an obsession, that I would go the way
of Lou Gehrig, the Iron Horse. No one told me
don't overdo it. Even if they had, I would've been
swinging at the scallops, bashing the bivalves.
Wanna have a good cry? For decades I had flashbacks
I was having another psychotic episode. *Fear and Trembling*:
isn't that a great title? I can't blame my parents or genes
(kinda refreshing). May I free myself, like Insight
Timer instructs, of debris. May I hover like a gull.

Not sure where this is going, though, yeah
pretty fucking sure. Pretty not pretty as my
daughter would say, kinda shapeless and no
funeral please, no roses or potted begonias.
Please donate to trawling for fish instead of
netting, to Cornell Lab of Ornithology. When
I stack breaths, I'm reminded it ceases –
that's the Hurricane Debby of this thing:
weakening diaphragmatic storms. Inhalations
de-escalating. My nineteen-year-old self didn't
imagine this. I was learning bird calls, hermit thrush
and song sparrow. Keeping a list, but also wandering
the forest counting the decades forward, a human
life like alpine snow that seems it will never melt.

POEM ON MY SON'S TWENTY-THIRD BIRTHDAY

How far away it seems, I told him last night, over rainbow rolls and agedashi.
How I went into labor on a Wednesday. Three days of people saying
I wasn't, that it was weeks away. On Saturday, I called the doula.

She suggested we go to the zoo. Three hours later he was slipping out of me
like a five-pound bass. Wide-eyed and curious,
he took a good look at us. Then he cried,

went for my breast. I didn't know how tired and anxious I'd get, how sure
someone would call CPS, how I'd panic when I couldn't stop his crying
even while belting out "Maxwell's Silver Hammer."

The night I ended up at Behavioral Health, my son in a squad car
because I said I wasn't sure, when they asked,
if I'd hurt him.

It was October. We'd pasted black bats on our front door,
strung candy-corn lights. I began hearing crows
that weren't there. Little boy in his blue fleecy.

Your dad brought you each afternoon during visiting hour,
where I held you, not sure I'd ever get out. My *now*
was committed. My mind, though doing better,

had spent a week hearing my father in the hallway, believing God,
the Unabomber, and I were in cahoots. But it turned out
to be hormonal. Soon I was taking him to mom

and baby yoga. We had a little routine, me-n-you: mornings on the go,
then home for your nap, then playing in the backyard, which morphed
to museums and zoos, to preschool

and school, two graduations, to this day I'm not telling you,
as I'm placing twenty-three candles on your cake, I spent four weeks
away from you because they thought I'd kill you.

Because I thought I was smoldering in a can like the ones they filled with wood,
set on fire beside a frozen Tommy's Pond.
What did that month end up mattering?

Less than this sip of sake I drink from your cup, less than this dab of wasabi
on my hamachi, less than this moment,
which leads to the next.

A POEM ABOUT TWINFLOWER

because my daughter says it's her favorite flower.
Because the blooms smell sweet—pale pink,
nodding bells. Because it grows

in moist, shady woods. Because the inflorescence
is trumpet-shaped like a pair of dangly earrings.
That she and I are paired too.

That being her mother is not to be her twin
but to be, at times, her creeping vine,
her comfort mat

of evergreen. That it grows in the mountains, the hikes
to Buckhorn Lake and Constance Pass,
where we found them beneath

hemlock and silver fir, among starflower,
lupine and pentstemon, heart-leaved arnica.
Where we pitched our tents,

where during the night we saw Jupiter, Saturn, and Mars.
Because this flower reminds me we will always
be dangling from the same stem,

that mothers and daughters are perennial. Blooming all summer,
dormant under snow, returning each June,
alongside club moss and deer fern,

in the cool dark forest where her body's half her father's,
half mine, but also all hers, where long-running stems
adhere us to the fragrant ground.

MY NINETEEN-YEAR-OLD DAUGHTER IS MY PERSONAL ASSISTANT,

learning what I need, what I need most. What I'm paying her for
mostly is having her in my arms, stroking her hair
because I don't know how much longer.

Is bringing me overnight oats with a dollop of yogurt,
a few smashed raspberries on top, with a label
that says "I LOVE YOU" in red marker.

Is watching three episodes of *Girls,* trying to decide
which character we like most—Hannah or Shosh,
or maybe Hannah's boyfriend Adam,

whom we hated at first (he peed on her in the shower!),
but who, by the end of Season 2, seems way less gross
and full of himself, wisdom-y

about romantic love. Is bingeing on rom-coms
with formulaic plots that always end
with a car, boat, or plane chase

to tell the woman *I love you*, which always makes me cry,
but a good kind of cry, ya know? Is when she asks
for a list of tasks, and at the top is *Come say hi,*

and tell me how you are (sweeping and mopping be damned!).
Is *Sit with me on the chaise,* listening to a scrub jay,
though we cannot see it,

though we don't know exactly where it is, how long
it will be there doing its weirdly scratchy
yet somehow melodious call.

YOU ARE MUCH MORE THAN THIS BODY

~ Thích Nhất Hạnh

which is really good to know because these days
this body isn't the electric eel it once was, isn't
sputtering like bacon or fizzing like a Coke,

is more like a salt lick without the salt, a bunch of wasps
on a vacation from buzzing. I'm no longer busy
like sugar ants in a left-out-by-mistake

tin of Fussie Cat, but I'm learning to notice lichen (wildly
chartreuse), the trunks of madrone, their breast-ish
protuberances. Also, a bush with both berries

and buds, and I liked that news—that we could be done fruiting,
last season's puckered maroon, but also, check it out,
little green shoots! I liked the way the wind

was making a mess of the water, the way a merganser gave up
on it altogether, settled on a rock to wait it out. Maybe
I'm waiting it out. Maybe saying hello

to my guardian angels—my mom, her mom, my Aunt Gloria—
is a good thing to do as I watch a piece of grass twirl.
Maybe, like Hạnh says, I need to adjust

to not having a lifespan, a self, a birth or death date. It's a lot
to accept: that we're *life without boundaries.*
The oak tree is the oak tree, he says,

but it's also the seed it was, though where's the freaking acorn?
That little nut is gone. It's like that part of ourselves
that will always be that kid doing cartwheels.

What's so great about going back into the void? As I shared with a friend,
we wouldn't be here without exploding stars,
so I guess it's best to focus on the clouds,

how fast or slow they're moving, the calamity
caused by wind, new leaves among
the dying fruit.

AUTHOR BIO:

Martha Silano's previous poetry collections include *Terminal Surreal* (Acre Books, 2025), *This One We Call Ours,* Winner of the 2023 Blue Lynx Prize (Lynx House Press, 2024). *Gravity Assist* (Saturnalia Books, 2019), *Reckless Lovely* (Saturnalia Books, 2014), and *The Little Office of the Immaculate Conception* (Saturnalia Books, 2011), winner of the Saturnalia Books Poetry Prize and a Washington State Book Award finalist. She is also co-author, with Kelli Russell Agodon, of *The Daily Poet: Day-by-Day Prompts for Your Writing Practice* (Two Sylvias Press, 2013). Martha's poems have appeared in *Poetry, Paris Review, American Poetry Review, Kenyon Review, The Missouri Review,* and in many anthologies, including *Cascadia: A Field Guide Through Art, Ecology, and Poetry* (Mountaineers Books, 2023), *Dear America: Letters of Hope, Habitat, Defiance, and Democracy* (Trinity University Press, 2019), and the *Best American Poetry* series (Norton, 2009). Awards include *North American Review's* James Hearst Poetry Prize and *The Cincinnati Review's* Robert and Adele Schiff Poetry Prize.

Martha Silano passed away from ALS in 2025.

ACKNOWLEDGMENTS

Gracious thanks to the editors of the following magazines for publishing the new poems, some in slightly different versions.

Bracken: "What Isn't Broken"
Broadsided Press: "I'm Not Sure Why I Decided"
The Cincinnati Review: "Eat, Prey, Love"
Colorado Review: "Dashing"
DIAGRAM: "Buying and Selling"
Diode: "And the road is like a cave with yellow walls"
The Florida Review: "Fondest Memories from the Locked Ward"
Grist: "Song"
The Inflectionist Review: "The Vital Question"
Italian Americana: "When This Boat My Body"
Kestrel: "Ars Poetica"
Laurel Review: "I sold my predicates,"
The McNeese Review: "The Weeds"
The Manhattan Review: "Postpartum Psychosis"
Mom Egg Review: "For My Daughter on Her Eighteenth Birthday" and "The Whole Vagina Experience"
MORIA: "The Doe Outside Our Back Door"
New England Review: "When I began to dig"
Pedestal: "Poetry," and "What I Wished For"
Plume Poetry: "I was trying to weigh darkness"
River & Sound Review: "Why I'd Like to Meet My Maker"
The Shore: "The Blooming"
Silk Road: "In Another Life"
Sixth Finch: "The Precise Mode of Failure Could Not be Replicated,"
Southern Indiana Review: "Just Don't Think About Waterfalls"
Sugar House Review: "Now We Come to Ticks and Tocks"
Superstition Review: "What is too much"

Sweet: A Literary Confection: "The Signs Were Clear"
SWWIM Every Day: "When wispy clouds drift through sparsely wooded mountains"
Third Coast: "And Yet It Moves"
Ucity Review "Blessed Are They That Mourn"
Whale Road Review: "Last Train to Paradise"

Selections from Terminal Surreal (Acre Books, 2025), courtesy Acre Books.
Selections from Terminal Surreal (Two Sylivias, 2015), courtesy Two Sylvias Press.
Selections from Terminal Surreal (Lynx House, 2024), courtesy Lynx House Press.
Selections from Terminal Surreal (Steel Toe Press, 2006), courtesy Steel Toe Press.

POEMS IN ANTHOLOGIES:

""The Bald Eagles of Seward Park," in *Birdbrains: A Lyrical Guide to the Birds of Washington State*, co-edited by Susan Rich, Hiroko Seki, and Dr. Stephanie Delaney. Raven Chronicles 2025.

"There's so much to Admire" in *Three Hearts: An Anthology of Cephalopod Poetry*. Sierra Nelson, anthology editor, Lana Hechtman Ayers, Managing Editor Concrete Wolf Press. April 2024.

Martha Silano's previous poetry collections include *Terminal Surreal* (Acre Books, 2025), *This One We Call Ours,* Winner of the 2023 Blue Lynx Prize (Lynx House Press, 2024). *Gravity Assist* (Saturnalia Books, 2019), *Reckless Lovely* (Saturnalia Books, 2014), and *The Little Office of the Immaculate Conception* (Saturnalia Books, 2011), winner of the Saturnalia Books Poetry Prize and a Washington State Book Award finalist. She is also co-author, with Kelli Russell Agodon, of *The Daily Poet: Day-by-Day Prompts for Your Writing Practice* (Two Sylvias Press, 2013). Martha's poems have appeared in *Poetry, Paris Review, American Poetry Review, Kenyon Review, The Missouri Review,* and in many anthologies, including *Cascadia: A Field Guide Through Art, Ecology, and Poetry* (Mountaineers Books, 2023), *Dear America: Letters of Hope, Habitat, Defiance, and Democracy* (Trinity University Press, 2019), and the *Best American Poetry* series (Norton, 2009). Awards include *North American Review*'s James Hearst Poetry Prize and *The Cincinnati Review*'s Robert and Adele Schiff Poetry Prize.

WHEN I LEARN CATASTROPHICALLY

is an anagram of *amyotrophic lateral sclerosis*.
When I learn I probably have a couple years,
maybe (catastrophically) less, crossword puzzles
begin to feel meaningless, though not the pair
of buffleheads, not the red cardinal of my heart.
The sky does all sorts of marvelously uncatastrophic
things that winter I shimmy between science
& song, between widgeons & windows, weather
& its invitation to walk. Walking, which becomes
my *lose less*, my *less morsels*, my *lose smile*
while *more sore looms*. Sometimes I wander
for hours, my mile pace over half an hour,
everyone passing the lady at dusk talking
to herself about *looming rooms, soil lies, ire
& else*. Chuckling about my mileage gone down
the toilet, I plant the *rose* of before, the *oil* of after.
As each breath elevates to miracle, I become
both more & less of who I'd been, increasingly
less concerned about the dishes in the sink,
more worried about the words in my notebooks,
all those unfinished poems. I remember the fear
of getting lost if I left the main trail. I remember
molehills, actual molehills, piles of salty roe,
mountains of limes. Catastrophically, it's rare:
one in 500,000, but then I learned the odds
of being born: one in 42 billion, though not sure
how they calculate, or the chances of the cosmos
having just the right amount of force to not
break apart. *Less smiles. More lose. Miser miles.*
A sis & bro whom I'll leave like a sinking island,

wished for? Had it been Venice,
the Uffizi, one more hike to Mason Lake,
Spiraea douglasii along its shore?

All of it, of course, all of it in unison,
that scent of early decay, that first
turn from summer to fall.

PREVIOUS BOOKS:

Terminal Surreal (Acre Books, 2025).

This One We Call Ours (Lynx House Press, 2024)

Gravity Assist (Saturnalia Books, 2019)

Reckless Lovely (Saturnalia Books, 2014)

What the Truth Tastes Like, expanded second edition (Two Sylvias Press, 2015)

The Daily Poet: Day-by-Day Prompts for Your Writing Practice (Two Sylvias Press, 2013).

The Little Office of the Immaculate Conception (Saturnalia Books, 2011)

Blue Positive (Steel Toe Books, 2006).

What the Truth Tastes Like (Nightshade Press, 1998)

Last Train to Paradise was printed in Adobe Garamond
www.saturnaliabooks.org

www.ingramcontent.com/pod-product-compliance
Lightning Source LLC
Chambersburg PA
CBHW060514080526
44586CB00012B/486